BEST DAYS *with* SHETLAND'S BIRDS

BEST DAYS *with* SHETLAND'S BIRDS

EDITED by

ANDREW HARROP & REBECCA NASON

The Shetland Times Ltd.
Lerwick
2022

BEST DAYS with SHETLAND'S BIRDS

ISBN 978-1-910997-47-5 Hardback
ISBN 978-1-910997-45-1 Paperback

First published by The Shetland Times Ltd., 2022.

Cover illustration: Windy day at Sumburgh Head ©Howard Towll

A catalogue record for this book is available from the British Library.

Printed and published by
The Shetland Times Ltd.,
Gremista, Lerwick,
Shetland ZE1 0PX, UK.

"It is very remarkable that a bird [thick-billed warbler] with so distant a range should stray so far to the west as the very edge of maritime Europe – yet it is by no means the first to have done so, and experience tells us that it will not be the last."

(Williamson 1965)

Contents

Pine grosbeak (*Pinicola enucleator*), Collafirth, February 2013, © Rebecca Nason.

Autumn

Winter

Foreword

I first visited Shetland in 1975. A chance conversation in a London pub had got me the post of assistant cook in the Fair Isle Bird Observatory. After a couple of days enforced stay in Mainland because of stormy weather, I took the *Good Shepherd* to the isle, and once I'd recovered from horrendous seasickness, I fell in love. With the island, its people and the sense of community that had brought the entire population to the haven to unload the boat.

At that point the birds and the dedicated staff who monitored breeding species and migrants were a total mystery. How was it possible to identify a small brown individual after a fleeting glimpse before it disappeared in a hole in the dyke? Why did prolonged westerly winds send the wardens and visitors into a state of deep depression, relieved only by endless games of bird name scrabble? And how could the arrival of a rarity make everyone so euphoric? My days were spent cleaning bathrooms, peeling tatties and visiting the islanders to listen to their stories of gales and shipwrecks and sheep. I didn't care much about the real work of the observatory.

But then it was spring and there were seabirds on the cliffs. Of course, even I fell for the puffins, and I came to tell the difference between kittiwakes and fulmars, guillemots and razorbills. I learned to stick one hand in the air in the hope that the diving Arctic skuas on the hill would aim for that and not for my head. Some evenings when the wardens were out to ring storm petrels or whooper swans, I'd go too, writing down ring numbers, sharing the excitement. I started to understand the thrill of a bird that was new for the isle, or for Shetland, or for the UK. Later, I met Tim whose enthusiasm was more contagious than Covid. I never became a birder, but I could understand his elation after a good day's birding.

I love the format of this book because it shares those moments of passion and excitement. This is no dry examination of facts or statistics. It helps us to understand the joy to be found in the natural world. These are the stories told and retold, while sheltering inside during westerly gales and horizontal rain. They're much more interesting than bird name scrabble!

Fair Isle, and later the rest of Shetland, taught me that nature is an intrinsic part of landscape. To fall in love with a place, without an understanding of the wildlife inhabiting or visiting it, is a limited kind of affection. The accounts of very special birding days, give us a real and wider sense of these beautiful islands.

Ann Cleeves

Acknowledgments

Paul Harvey and Roger Riddington encouraged us to pursue this project from its inception, and offered helpful advice. All the authors, artists (Paul Bloomer and Howard Towll) and photographers (John Coutts, Larry Dalziel, David Gifford, Lee Gregory, Jack Levene, George Petrie and Jonathan Wills, as well as those listed as authors) have contributed freely and supported the donation of royalties from sales of the book to Shetland Bird Club. Ann Cleeves kindly contributed the Foreword. We are proud that so many in the Shetland birding community have joined forces in this way, all bound by their love of birds and a desire to help Shetland's birdlife through supporting the Shetland Bird Club, a strong club which dates back to 1973.

Our publisher The Shetland Times Ltd, in particular Charlotte Black as publications manager, helped with technical advice and brought the project to fruition. Being produced and printed locally means a lot to us, personally and environmentally.

Partners and family, not only of the editors but also of the authors, artists and photographers, have shown understanding of the demands made by studying birds, often at unsocial hours, and tolerance whilst we delivered personal, heartfelt accounts, images and art for this publication. Special mention must go to our respective partners, Eleanor Pottinger and Phil Harris, for long-standing support, good counsel and a sense of perspective.

We have tried to ensure that the accounts collected here are a true representation of birdwatching in Shetland. Any errors which remain are the responsibility of the editors.

Editors' Introduction

"Today was the greatest birding day of my life." So wrote Iain Davies on 28th May 2018 after counting an estimated 721,620 warblers passing through Tadoussac, Quebec, Canada. Experiences in Shetland are very different, but can be equally profound. The authors of the accounts included here have all, in their different ways, articulated what Shetland's birds mean to them and some of their best days. One way or another, they have all dedicated a large part of their lives to watching or studying birds and care deeply about their conservation.

The concept of 'Best Days' in Shetland goes back at least as far as the discovery of Fair Isle as a magnet for migrants. Writing an account of 23rd September 1908, Eagle Clarke described it as: "the best bird day for autumn as yet". His log included:

"A number of Red-spotted Bluethroats (adults and young). These birds were, with one exception, found in potatoes or turnips. They ran with the rapidity of a Partridge along the drills, sometimes for a hundred yards, until they reached the end of the cover; then with a rapid flight they doubled back and repeated their tactics. They are dark like a Hedge-Accentor [Dunnock] on the wing, and the bay-red tail is not so conspicuous as one would suppose. One of the birds was found by the side of a small stream, a haunt much resorted to, where there was little or no cover; and it ran under a stone for concealment, which is also a common habit."

Not to be outdone, Mary, Duchess of Bedford excelled herself on 14th May 1910:

"In a stream by one of the little Mill houses, I thought I caught sight of another Bluethroat, but the fog was so thick that I could not follow it. However, very shortly after I saw one settling on a stone wall and shot it. It proved to be a Red-spotted Bluethroat. Much elated at my success, I started on the rather hopeless mission of trying to find Mr. Eagle Clarke in the fog. I returned to the ditch where I had fired at the Bluethroat in the morning, and to my surprise found it again. As there is always the chance of a White-spotted Bluethroat, I fired again and killed it. To my great satisfaction I found it was a White-spotted Bluethroat, the fifth recorded for Great Britain, two of which have now been obtained in Fair Isle. My shot brought up Mr. Eagle Clarke, and I had the satisfaction of showing him Red- and White-spotted Bluethroats shot within half an hour of each other – the one a Central European breeding bird, the other a Northern European breeding species. About 7pm the fog cleared off, and though very footsore and weary, I once more trudged to the Mill. I put up a Kestrel, which we have not yet seen here, and which made the twenty-fourth migrant I have seen to-day. Once more I came across another Bluethroat. I returned to Ortolan Cottage [Pund] at 8.10pm, having been on the hunt for ten hours, but I have been well rewarded, as I doubt whether many people can claim to have seen such rare birds in the British Islands in one day as: 3 Red-spotted Bluethroats, 1 White-spotted Bluethroat, 2 Ortolan Buntings, 1 Hoopoe."

The days described in this book encompass a wide variety of experiences over two generations. Some could be replicated by those fortunate to be in the right place at the right time, others are likely to remain unique. In Shetland as elsewhere, even the natural soundtracks of our youth have changed: for example, you can no longer hear Manx shearwaters anywhere in Shetland, whilst the number and variety of singing passerines in Shetland's plantations has increased.

The decade or so of the oil boom (evocatively portrayed by Jamieson 1986) created new possibilities but also new problems. Disasters such as the *Esso Bernicia* oil spill were obvious enough, but few foresaw the impact that our dependence on fossil fuels would have on the global climate. Probably, even those like the 'oil boom birders' with a deep interest in wildlife thought they'd never had it so good.

The people of Shetland and the birds of Shetland need one another more than ever. Despite worrying declines in many bird populations, there are examples which give us hope: some of Shetland's iconic breeding birds, including red-necked phalaropes, merlins and red-throated divers are holding their own; and numbers of some migrant passerines from the east, notably yellow-browed warblers, have increased. Many people are involved in watching, counting, studying and protecting these birds. We hope that future generations will be inspired to do the same.

Andrew Harrop and Rebecca Nason
Shetland, December 2021

Map of Shetland

Rediscovering Albert

27th March 1990
Mike Pennington

The Shetland winter is long and dark. Although the days lengthen in the New Year and the shalders (oystercatchers) return in February, spring can take a long time to establish itself. March is often a windy month, but 27th March 1990 was one of those calm, steely-grey, overcast days which tempt out the brave for their first long walk of the year. I decided to go to Hermaness and see if the bonxies had returned and look around the nature reserve.

On arrival, a flock of noisy shalders flew across from the Burrafirth links, piping vehemently. A few skylarks and meadow pipits, also newly returned from mainland Britain where they shelter from the worst of the Shetland winter storms, flitted across the heather. In mid-winter, Hermaness really is a barren place, with barely a bird to share the place with the wind-blasted sheep, but spring is slowly drawing them back to their breeding places.

After the initial stony ascent above the car park, you emerge on a plateau of sodden blanket bog which acts like a huge sponge through the winter, soaking up the rain as the peat and the sphagnum moss expand. Each footstep squelches into the damp peat leaving an oozing, bubbling trail behind a walker. Occasional hollows of engorged, vivid, iridescent green sphagnum lurk waiting to trap the incautious walker who tries to cross them. Soggy feet are only half of the problem on a blanket bog – soggy legs are just as likely. Nevertheless, there is something rather magnificent about the bleak sweep of wind-burnt brown heather topped by the Shetland sky, which somehow always contrives to be busier, moodier, and bigger than skies anywhere else in the world.

Sothers on the west coast of Hermaness, nestling between the higher points of the Neap and Hermaness Hill, is always one of my favourite destinations. In the summer it is the home of thousands of puffins, which will regard their human visitors with as much curiosity as we regard them, but it is a little early for them to have returned from their hard, lonely winter in the mid-Atlantic. I scan the sea with binoculars, hoping an early arrival is bobbing on the sea waiting to come ashore – but no luck. Perhaps there will be some this evening, as the first arrivals usually come ashore for the first time at dusk.

A whistle of wings and a muted trumpet call alert me to a flock of whooper swans – 33 of them beating steadily into a freshening northwest wind. What are they doing here? There are no large bodies of water on Hermaness, while 33 is a very large flock for

Shetland in spring. The birds head out to sea over the cliffs. A few hundred metres offshore they circle once, as if to confirm their position, or perhaps to help stiffen the resolve of the weaker members of the group, then they head off northwest again. I realise that this is a flock passing through Shetland, perhaps from Scotland, on its way back to Iceland to breed. I watch as their startling white gradually disappears into the pale grey above the horizon. In ten or twelve hours they will be honking in triumph as they cross the last of the grey Atlantic and return to Iceland. Some journey.

The wind is picking up from the west, allowing the maalies to perform in the updraft of the cliffs. Maalies, or fulmars, are not always the most popular birds as they defend themselves by spitting stomach oil and their previous meal at intruders, and they wouldn't win any avian beauty contest, but few birds can master the air as they can. They hang almost motionless in the updrafts at the top of the cliffs, with just tiny adjustments of their wings, before swooping down in swift ecstatic glides. It is hard to watch them and not believe that they are flying for the pure fun of it.

I scan Hermaness Hill, capital of the Hermaness bonxie kingdom, and usually the first place to be occupied by returning birds. A bonxie soars into view, as expected: at that time they seemed to arrive in the last few days of March almost without fail, although they tend to be a little later these days. 150 years ago, Hermaness was one of only a handful of places in Britain where the bonxie, or great skua, could be seen, but there are now the best part of 1,000 pairs on Hermaness alone. Like the maalie, bonxies are not popular birds – hanging around lambing yows and eating puffins endear them to neither crofter nor tourist, while their vigorous defence of their nest, which might engender praise or respect in a more photogenic species, adds to their malicious public profile. It is strange how lions or orcas are hailed as magnificent predators, yet bonxies are typified as cruel bullies. In one of nature's little ironies, Shetland's bonxie population is the most important in the world, despite their unpopularity.

The day has changed. The wind has picked up and there is now the promise of rain in the air. The cliffs' feet are wrapped in white blankets of surf as the waves hammer relentlessly at the rocks. But it is still not time to return home. Too many days cooped inside in the winter, or gritting teeth into even fiercer gales than this, makes this a day to relish and enjoy. Time to turn up the collar and dig the woolly hat out of the coat pockets and climb the Neap, Hermaness's highest point. A couple of snow buntings are there, foraging in the clifftop sward, staggering sideways in the gusts of wind or flitting in a sudden blizzard of white wings to a new, more sheltered, spot.

From the top of the Neap, Yell is already disappearing into the menacing charcoal clouds, while Ronas Hill, which looms on the horizon on clearer days, has long since disappeared from view. Out of habit I lift my binoculars to look across to the cliff at Saito, to where the famous Hermaness albatross used to sit, although not since my arrival on the island. Buffeted, and with my eyes streaming due to the increasing wind, I can hardly believe what I can see: a large black and white bird is sitting on Albert's ledge. No, surely not, it must be a black-back, I tell myself. But it's got an enormous yellow bill, the logical side of my brain tells me, and it's bigger than the gannets.

I find a spot to lie down out of the wind; it's drier here on the clifftop away from the peat, if that matters. I'm right – it is Albert, he's back, after an absence of almost three years. Back to take up his lonely vigil waiting for another black-browed albatross, as lost as he is, to find him amongst the thousands of gannets, the best he can find for company. Where has he been these last three years? What made him decide to return? How long will he stay this time? How do I get closer to get a better look at him? What a bird, one of those legendary birds you never believe you're going to see for yourself in real life, not in Britain, but here is one sitting on a cliff in Shetland, glancing round imperiously at the surrounding gannets.

The walk back seems to take ages – I can't wait to let people know that he's back – but this is another Unst day to remember, alongside the endless light of simmer dim, the noisy excitement of the summer seabird colonies, the occasional hordes of autumn migrants blown off course by grey south-easterly gales, the magnificence of the awesome winter seas following a storm, or the glorious but frustratingly infrequent days of intense blue skies when the beaches look like the Caribbean without palm trees.

Out Skerries

30th March 2000
Roger Riddington

After almost 30 years of living and working in Shetland, I have a plethora of 'best birding days' to pick from. There have been so many unexpected rarities, so many good days of migrant hunting in spring and autumn. Yet there have been so many special days with seabirds too. Moreover, now that retirement gives me greater options for time in the field, I have every hope that more memorable days with migrants lie ahead. For a variety of reasons, I suspect that my best days with seabirds will not be repeated.

I set foot in Shetland for the first time on 18th April 1992. During the course of a blisteringly cold long weekend I saw pine grosbeak, black-browed albatross and snowy owl (in that order) and undertook a superficial exploration of some of the islands that subsequently became home. None of that prepared me for the Tuesday after that long weekend, and the worst boat journey in my whole life, ever. After two and three-quarter hours of unremitting misery in the bowels of *Good Shepherd IV*, I staggered ashore in Fair Isle. I was the seabird assistant warden in 1992, a year when Fair Isle's seabird populations were still bountiful (although even then some were already in decline): for example, 18,159 pairs of kittiwakes and 109 pairs of Arctic skuas in 1992 compares with 859 and 28 respectively in the most recent all-island surveys, in 2015 and 2019. The sight, sound and smell of packed seabird colonies was exhilarating, and made a lasting impression. In fact, the whiff of spring guillemot takes me back to 1992 in an instant. The populations of many of Shetland's seabirds have dwindled steadily over the past 30 years, apparently mainly because of a changing climate and the impact of that on the distribution and abundance of key species of fish prey. Broadly, the species which are more catholic in their diet or can travel large distances to forage (gannet, fulmar, storm petrel) still thrive; species that need to find food closer to their breeding colonies (kittiwakes, terns, Arctic skuas) do not.

Another reason why my best days with seabirds are generally those from 20-odd years ago is, less intuitively, health and safety. No, really! In my four years as the warden of Fair Isle Bird Observatory (1994-97), the guidelines for what you would ask your staff to do were largely dictated by previous experience, tradition and common sense. Nowadays, the restrictions on fieldwork are, unsurprisingly, significantly greater (and this is an observation rather than a criticism): long trips in an inflatable boat with just a life jacket and extra petrol, or long descents of steep cliffs using just a tethered rope as a guide, are no longer permissible. Yet those days of summer seabird monitoring invoke such good memories.

I don't mind admitting that the Fair Isle's cliffs and seas frightened the life out of me initially, but I came to love them. Ringing expeditions to the teeming guillemot colonies at Lericum and Wester Lother, Sauversteen and Kuthin beach – places where the din from yelling adults and piping chicks was deafening – was such a privilege. Some of the climbing was hard work (especially if you were carrying one of the sections of aluminium ladder that we needed to reach the kittiwake ledges); and admittedly the point where I could easily scramble over the North Naaversgill overhang has surely long passed, health and safety or not. The routes that we used would all have been well-known to the Fair Islanders of years ago though. The crofters kept sheep on the iconic Sheep Rock for hundreds of years until the late 1970s, which entailed regular visits, hauling sheep up and down the precipitous access route on the seaward side. Yet, as far as I know, Sheep Rock was last climbed in my last year as warden, when my two assistants, Jenny Bull and Jane Reid, and I went up there on 31st July 1997 (to ring fulmars, not to round up sheep ...).

But my task for this book is to describe one day. On Thursday, 30th March, 2000, when my time in Fair Isle had come to an end and I'd moved out to mainland Shetland, the alarm woke me from a deep sleep at 3.30am. I was dressed and out of the door by 4.00, and soon after that I was in the smoke-filled cab of Martin Heubeck's Toyota pick-up, with a Zodiac inflatable lashed to the trailer behind. There was already light in the sky to the east and the day was cold with just a breath of westerly wind; calm seas are a prerequisite for counting seabirds from a boat. We motored steadily north from Dunrossness, bound for Vidlin, on the northeast coast of mainland Shetland. Jonathan Swale was the third member of the team and he was there to help us drag the Zodiac into the water and manhandle the two 25hp Suzuki outboards from their travelling position onto the boat's rear transom. The spare petrol cans were stowed and the boat box with emergency flares, VHF radio, coffee and sandwiches was strapped down. The good folk of Vidlin were still asleep as we nosed out of the marina at 5.45, but an overcast dawn had broken and there were plenty of seabirds on the water. Jonathan opened the throttles, the boat surged forward and we made rapid progress on an invitingly flat sea. We were heading east, past the north coast of Whalsay and on to the easternmost of the Shetland islands, the Out Skerries. Those islands will be known to many readers of this book mainly for their track record of rare migrants in autumn, but on that day in March 2000 the task in hand was to count the islands' population of tysties (black guillemots).

On fine mornings in early spring, tysties gather on the sea close to their breeding sites and for the first few hours of daylight most birds will be out on the water. A few will be perched beside their intended nest crevice and these birds need to be flushed onto the sea to join the others for a reliably accurate count. This is taken to be a good index of the population and there are stretches of the Shetland coastline covered every year by the SOTEAG (Shetland Oil Terminal Environmental Advisory Group) team in order to monitor population trends. The Skerries are not routinely covered though and, in fact, this was the first all-island count of tysties. So there was a pioneer element to our trip, which is always good for the soul. That survey was one of many dedicated boat trips in 1999 and 2000 to count the whole of Shetland's breeding seabird populations for a national survey – Seabird 2000 (written up in Mitchell *et al.* 2004). Sadly, at the time of writing, that is still the most recent complete survey of Shetland's seabirds.

Seabird 2000 was an opportunity for me to see many unfamiliar bits of the Shetland coastline from the sea. Back then we were unfettered by the guidelines of being within so many kilometres of a designated launchpad, and we had some long and memorable days out. It is hard to pick just one, but that circumnavigation of Skerries on 30th March 2000 somehow has special memories. The weather was cold, dull and overcast, with patchy drizzle, but count conditions were perfect. Our tally of 687 birds in breeding plumage comprised a little over four per cent of the Shetland total of 16,007 in Seabird 2000 (Pennington *et al*. 2004). Being the first Skerries count, we didn't really know what to expect, but for a fairly small area with relatively low cliffs such a high total was surprising. There were some memorable concentrations: as we edged slowly further into one of the two large geos on the east side of Mio Ness the birds kept pouring out, with a final count of 90 birds on the sea outside the geo.

I have always particularly enjoyed the tystie counts, which precede most of the year's seabird work and, indeed, spring migration: the whole season lies ahead. And it's hard to beat a tystie in spring finery; a winning combination of black and white plumage, with those gorgeous, deep crimson legs and bill linings, not to mention the high-pitched, slightly mournful calls, a harbinger of spring just as surely as the first song of skylark and blackbird, or the tumbling display of the lapwing. On our trip around Skerries that morning there were other distractions too – the first puffins of the year were back onshore; a tight flock of 100 purple sandpipers on Muckle Holm was notable, as was a distant peregrine; while on the way back to Vidlin we had nice views of an early Manx shearwater, disturbed from the sea surface by the boat. That Manxie was probably one of a handful of breeding birds that remained on Fetlar at the turn of the century; once a common breeding species, it is now considered extinct in the islands.

One of the joys of living in Shetland is that you never know when a truly special wildlife encounter is just around the corner. It might be something spectacular – a pod of killer whales, a family of otters, a snowy owl on a winter hill top or a white-tailed eagle heading north on a spring morning. Yet many of the commoner birds are equally special and, despite the downturn in numbers of many species, days spent among Shetland's breeding seabirds are hard to beat.

Best days with Shetland's birds

24th April 2021

Joyce J. M. Garden

Spring and autumn migration undoubtedly can bring some of the best birding days in Shetland but birding success depends on the weather, particularly wind direction and force. Although spring is a comparatively short period of birding opportunity, many of the migrants are in breeding plumage with males indicating their presence, even in thick cover, by song. Falls of migrants provide memorable birding but, more often, spring passage can be sporadic with trickles of commoner migrants punctuated by an occasional rarity. Settled weather brings great viewing conditions, but fewer migrants as they overfly the islands. Autumn migration is more prolonged but the weather is frequently unpredictable and daylight hours are shorter. Moreover, many autumn migrants are first-winter birds which can be less easy to identify.

Birding is about being in the right place at the right time. Ticking off one rarity and then moving on to another is an exciting possibility but the reality is often more prosaic. It is about balance – should you stay and see what arrives in your local patch or travel elsewhere? Before you decide to travel a reasonable distance, you weigh up factors such as the chances of the bird remaining in the area, the opportunity of seeing it, ferry timetables and the weather forecast.

Different birders have different opinions on a really good birding day. For some, it can be watching a scarce migrant in their garden, for others it can be travelling from one end of Shetland to the other to see a rarity. Some enjoy the company of other like-minded birders; others prefer their own company. I enjoy seeing a 'lifer', such as my first Siberian rubythroat, or a first for Shetland, like the Siberian accentor. Being in Fair Isle during a 'fall' of spring migrants was an equally exhilarating experience.

However, for me, birding is also about observing and recording subtle changes such as bird behaviour, interactions and the cross-over of winter visitors and summer breeders. It is these ever-shifting dynamics of the seasons, peppered with the unexpected, which has provided some of my best birding days. Shetland lies at the crossroads of the north-south and east-west migration routes but it is also the northernmost part of the range for some species and the southernmost for others.

A day in late April 2021 illustrates this. It started off with a fine, second-calendar-year Iceland gull in Lerwick. Watching this visitor from Greenland, with its pale plumage and pinkish dark-tipped bill, I was reminded of the unprecedented influx of 400 of these gulls in January 2012, when 50 were recorded at the Shetland Catch. As I observed this lone gull, I remembered the area festooned with hungry Iceland gulls, driven south by food shortages.

Shetland has approximately 1,450km of varied coastline with sheltered shorelines providing a magnet for birds in all seasons. Our next stop was the sheltered voe at Boddam where the rocky shore was sprinkled with a flock of around 30 turnstone. Displaying smart rusty-ginger, black and white plumage, these stocky waders were on their way north to breed in the high Arctic. A wheatear, a common summer breeding visitor, perched on a fence post after arriving from wintering in Africa whilst a huddle of oystercatchers were displaying and piping loudly. A male mallard sailed past and a black-headed gull swooped over the voe.

At the Pool of Virkie, the incoming tide had brought redshank, dunlin, curlew, knot and ringed plovers closer to the shore. Then a sparrowhawk flew low over the mudflats and the waders scattered, the knot forming a twisting, flashing silver-winged flock. However, six strikingly-plumaged shelduck remained, sifting the mud for small crustaceans. Shelduck breed in Shetland in very small numbers. I recalled an evening, a few years ago, watching 10 fluffy shelduck ducklings, accompanied by their parents, being led down to the shoreline as the sun set.

We moved on to the West Voe of Sumburgh, its aqua-turquoise waters glittering in the sunlight. Offshore were a flock of over 160 long-tailed ducks. Elegant, common winter visitors, they would soon depart to breed in the high Arctic. Also foraging in the bay were several great northern divers with one in almost full summer plumage, transformed into a symphony of black and white. One of Shetland's iconic summer breeding birds, a red-throated diver, was also present. The surprised "aa-oohs" from courting male eiders drifted across the water. Turnstones and a few purple sandpipers, also Arctic breeders, perched on the rocks. A bonxie barrelled past, another returning summer breeder, whilst a single common tern appeared. Common terns are usually the first species of tern to arrive back in the islands. Another familiar call, a distinctive, rippling trill, heralded the fly-over of two whimbrel, a species with its breeding stronghold here.

Shetland offers some amazing opportunities to experience the sight, sound and smell of breeding seabird colonies. Sumburgh Head provides a mecca for birders and non-birders. Today the main attraction, the puffins, had gone fishing except for one individual at the mouth of its burrow. The crammed guillemot colony was in full swing, their growling calls echoing up the cliff face with pairs of razorbills in their spacious rock niches adding to the chorus. Fulmars were cackling to each other, occupying their nest sites many months prior to laying a single egg. Other seabirds included onomatopoeic kittiwakes, shags, black guillemots, great black-backed gulls and herring gulls, with the white crosses of gannets gliding past. All these species were now in the annual race to raise their broods successfully, many depending on an abundant supply of small fish.

Enjoying a coffee above the shimmering expanse of sea, with Fair Isle etched on the south horizon, word came through that a spoonbill was at Setter Marsh at the Loch of Spiggie. I had narrowly missed the last one in Brae, but this bird obligingly stayed put, providing great views of a local rarity. Along with several other birders, we enjoyed watching it foraging voraciously, stalking across the marsh into the shallow water, its feathery crest

Nightjar ***(Caprimulgus europaeus)*****, Bressay, May 2017, © Joyce Garden.**

blowing in the slight breeze. It swished its extraordinary bill from side to side, filtering out aquatic invertebrates. A fitting end to a day which illustrated the seasonal change-over in Shetland as well as the unexpected.

My late friend, Terry Rogers, disliked 'chasing after migrants'. Having spent years on weather ships and living abroad, he had a formidable bird list. His philosophy in Shetland was to 'bring the birds to him'. Around his house in Nesting, he designed and planted an amazing garden with coniferous and deciduous trees. Following his lead and encouragement, we also planted varied trees and shrubs which, as the garden has matured, have attracted a wide range of bird species over the years.

On one memorable day, first a great grey shrike touched down and then a wryneck. Another day, a ring ouzel appeared in a grassy patch and then flew up into the trees. Passerines in the garden have included willow warbler, chiffchaff, wood warbler, blackcap, garden warbler, reed warbler, lesser whitethroat, common whitethroat, barred warbler, icterine warbler, yellow-browed warbler and goldcrest along with pied, spotted and red-breasted flycatchers. We have observed finches such as hawfinch, goldfinch, chaffinch, brambling, greenfinch, bullfinch, siskin, common redpoll, common rosefinch, two-barred and common crossbills, twite and yellowhammer. Other visitors over the years have included wheatear, cuckoo, red-backed shrike, redwing, fieldfare, common redstart, robin, song thrush, dunnock, woodcock, mallard, meadow pipit, tree pipit, swallow, house martin, long-eared owl, hooded crow, common gull, great tit and great spotted woodpecker. Migrant and resident passerines attract predators. A sparrowhawk was a frequent visitor during winter 2020/21, perching in the trees menacingly, before pouncing on an unfortunate house sparrow. Also, brightening up the Covid-restricted season, were the regular visits of up to three wintering blue tits to the feeders. They also quickly learned to access food in the sanctuary cage feeder.

Watching birds in your garden has the advantage that shy, skulking species can be easily observed. Another visitor was a water rail which fiercely attacked any starling, blackbird, house sparrow or rock dove anywhere near where it was foraging. It was fascinating to see how its laterally-flattened body, designed for moving through thick cover, allowed it to squeeze through the bars of the sanctuary bird feeder.

However, vagrants have also occurred. One wet evening in May 2017 I noticed a cryptically coloured bird on a branch about 10 metres away from the window – a nightjar. The buff-white, brown, grey and black plumage, with mottling, streaking and barring, provided superb camouflage against the tree bark. At such close quarters, the large head, short neck and small bill were clearly visible. It was a privilege to observe such an unusual, nocturnal bird at close range for a prolonged period and to see it in flight the next day.

Vagrants, migrants, summer visitors, winter visitors, resident birds throughout Shetland and in my garden, make up my best days with Shetland's birds, blended into a cornucopia of observing, learning, recording, enjoyment and appreciation.

Fair Isle

27th April 2014
David Parnaby

'Best day's birding in Shetland'? Having been warden of the Fair Isle Bird Observatory for over 10 years, it's not an immediately easy choice. There are some absolutely stand-out birds, either for their rarity, sheer beauty or circumstances: a famous Sunday evening magnolia warbler twitch; carrying my shoeless then seven-year-old daughter Grace across Buness to twitch a distant black-browed albatross which then appeared right above our heads; a 'honking' bridled tern mobbing me during Arctic tern nest counts on Buness (the only time I've been left speechless by finding a bird; the rest of the team had to interpret my points and grunts); the challenge of a dull green warbler in the hand (and a much brighter one whilst buying ice creams a few years later); hurriedly learning about what makes a glaucous-winged gull; eastern olivaceous and river warbler in the Obs nets at the same time; being alone with a positively shimmering male Siberian rubythroat as it fed a few metres away from me; finding my first British hoopoe on the day my daughter Freyja was born . . . the list is almost endless. Then there are the fall days, with birds everywhere; either swarms of autumn thrushes across the isle, or a colourful spring migrant in every geo. Not forgetting the breeding birds: a full day in the Obs boat counting seabirds on the cliffs and exploring bits of Fair Isle that most people never get to see takes some beating, as do some of the epic storm petrel ringing nights (especially those that end up with three species of petrel being caught!).

In the end, I've chosen a classic spring day with a slowly building arrival of birds, a scattering of rarities, topped with two with less than 10 British records between them, all set against the backdrop of sharing it all with the FIBO team: a sizeable percentage of the enjoyment of birding for me is in sharing it with others.

Late April 2014 had seen a high pressure system deliver a fairly constant airflow all the way from southeast Europe and migrants had started to pass through. The 26th April had delivered a few year ticks and I got very excited about a gadwall – a Fair Isle tick for me no less. With a forecast for south-easterly winds on 27th April there were high hopes of being able to top that. Sure enough, the day felt very good from the off and assistant warden Ciaran Hatsell's pre-breakfast census of Buness finished with a short-toed lark and reed bunting dropping out of the sky together as he returned to the Obs.

There's nothing like an early morning rarity to get the excitement levels ramped up over the bacon and eggs and an optimistic team headed out into census with high hopes and most definitely a spring in the step. There was a decent array of birds on census: lingering western subalpine warbler, wryneck and great grey shrike, and a few common migrants dotted around, with the rarest new offering being a red-breasted flycatcher found by assistant warden Richard Cope at Burkle just before lunch. We returned to the Obs a happy bunch, not realising the knock-on effect that the RBF would have on the rest of the day.

Sunday lunch was an occasion not to be missed at FIBO and the day's menu was a typically delicious beef, roasties and all the trimmings. I finished mine in the office to follow Sunderland AFC's latest attempts at avoiding relegation and was more than pleasantly surprised at a four-nil win against Cardiff. A good day all round, and Sunday afternoon was the traditional half-day off a week, so a bit of digesting the substantial roast, some time with the family and maybe a bit more birding were all on the cards. I remember very clearly the moment all that changed though: I was still marvelling at the football when Deryk Shaw phoned to say he'd just photographed a male Cretzschmar's bunting! As it was so early in the season there weren't guests to gather, but the staff were summoned, news was phoned round the rest of the isle and we headed down to Burkle. It turned out that Deryk had gone to photograph the red-breasted flycatcher (a new bird for his croft), when the bunting had crept out of the grass in front of him. The point blank photos he showed us when we arrived were pretty amazing, but the news that it was no longer there was less so. It had flown round the back of his house, not looking like it had gone far but our searches became increasingly desperate as there was no further sign.

It was only the fifth British Cretzschmar's bunting, although the third for Fair Isle (where the first British records occurred in 1967 and 1979), so needless to say everyone was keen to catch up with it. The searching began; we split up to cover as wide an area as possible and tried to focus on anywhere that felt like it would be good for buntings. Still no sign of the Cretzschmar's but there were obviously more birds in; a fabled 'classic Fair Isle afternoon fall'. The time of year meant there was a broad range of species, with departing winter thrushes, snow buntings and finches mixing with warblers and chats. Flicking pied flycatchers, speezing tree pipits, shivering redstarts, bramblings nasally twiyeing, dozens of *Phylloscs* bouncing about, chacking flocks of fieldfares: it was great birding. I guess we should have felt disappointed at not relocating the Cretzschmar's, but the excitement of the birding was just too much: if you can't enjoy days like that, you should hang up your bins. At one point, Nick Riddiford attracted attention by blowing on a whistle and frantically waving – although it was for a short-toed lark near Midway, not what we were hoping for. A quick check of Buness showed the original short-toed lark was still there, whilst a third was found shortly after on Meoness. Blue-headed wagtail, a long-staying Kumlien's gull and an impressive seven wrynecks added to the scarcity haul.

After a six-hour afternoon of covering and re-covering the entire south of the isle, the light was fading, we were flagging and starting to bird back towards the Obs. Passing the Meadow Burn, a bird flicked up onto the fence near the 'reed box', a male stonechat, but a very pale one. Although it was distant, it fanned its tail as it landed on the wire, displaying a 'wheatear' tail pattern. A Caspian stonechat! The rest of the team and other birders were soon on the scene and the bird not only obliged, it followed the fence lines until eventually passing within a couple of metres of everyone. Just the fifth record of this distinctive subspecies for Britain, it was a cracking consolation for the lack of the Cretzschmar's and summed up a lot of what is special about birding Fair Isle. Log followed a delayed dinner (a fitting meze-style meal considering the origin of the birds) and revealed the variety and numbers of species, resulting in almost certainly the best April day's birding in Fair Isle's long history.

Cretzschmar's bunting *(Emberiza caesia)*, Fair Isle, April 2014, © Deryk Shaw.

Caspian stonechat (*Saxicola maurus variegatus*), Fair Isle, April 2014 © Deryk Shaw.

It's only meant to be a best day, but as a postscript, it's worth mentioning that a forensic search of all the areas and similar habitats utilised by Fair Isle's previous Cretzschmar's buntings the following day was eventually abandoned, but the bird then turned up on census allowing everyone good views (and a large twitch when a steady stream of twitchers from across the UK came to see it). The celebrations that night were almost certainly at least partially responsible for the wardening team missing Fair Isle's second mandarin the following morning. As a further postscript, the spring went on to produce calandra lark, hermit thrush, collared flycatcher, laughing gull and three firsts for Fair Isle (glossy ibis, bridled tern and Moltoni's warbler) and set the year up nicely for a total of 221 species, a record haul for the isle.

As a final postscript (I promise), a perhaps more typical late April birding day followed on the first anniversary of the Cretzschmar's sighting, with Log for that day noting cold, snowy showers and vicious hail storms, and the day's birding highlight consisted of a long-staying mute swan!

Pomarine skuas off Wats Ness

9th May 1992
Hugh Harrop and Mick Mellor

On 8th May 1992 news was broadcast on the birders' grapevine that Dave Suddaby had seen over 400 pomarine skuas off Wats Ness. At the time this was an amazing number for Shetland, easily the highest day total recorded, giving us the encouragement to get up early the next morning and head out to this remote West Mainland location. The weather forecast predicted similar conditions for the following day: strong north-westerly winds with frequent showers of rain, snow, and hail.

The forecasters were correct and on 9th May, along with Martin Heubeck, we trudged from our vehicles the half a mile or so to be on the low cliffs at Watsness by 6.00am, armed with binoculars, telescopes and tripods. Appropriately dressed in layers of thermals, T-shirts and jumpers, with an outer layer of coats, waterproofs, and wellies, we had enough food and coffee to last us a few hours, but little did we know that eleven hours later we (HH and MM) would be staggering back to the car feeling sunburnt, hypothermic, dehydrated and thoroughly exhausted.

Once in position we sat patiently scanning the sea waiting for something to happen; eventually a flock of four pomarine skuas flew north at close range, almost following the cliffs. This was almost one hour later, and we had started to question the wisdom of our decision. However, this was followed by a gradual increase in sightings up until the early afternoon, when we had reached the enviable total of 472 pomarine skuas, with the biggest flock noted being 82. This was just a trickle compared to what was to come.

As time passed there was a steady flow of Shetland birdwatchers until there was quite a crowd trying to shelter from the onslaught of the frequent snow and hail showers. It was an exciting time as we scoured the waves in search of skuas amid the urgent shouts from different observers, and their varying attempts to locate pointers to make sure the whole group did not miss any. Foula became a particularly useful landmark for this purpose. At some time in the afternoon Martin had to leave; he encouraged us with his departing words being something like, "You might get to a thousand today".

This spectacular movement occurred in two major waves, involving an increase in sightings up until early afternoon, followed by a lull (with occasional distant small numbers only) during a period of sunny weather, which felt almost tropical in comparison to what we had endured earlier in the day. It was during this lull in skua migration, when we were the only two observers left on the cliffs, that we contemplated giving up due to the lack of birds, as well as a lack of sustenance, but our determination took over. "Give it another fifteen minutes," was a recurring comment, until a huge black cloud signalled the approach of another shower. The second wave began at 2.45pm, just after a shower, and continued at a faster rate and in greater numbers than during the first wave.

Fortunately, we stayed put. During this second wave we amassed an incredible total of 1,350 pomarine skuas in just over two hours.

Midway through the second wave, the bigger flocks were observed at a height of several hundred feet, some of these were picked out as mere dots high up over the horizon. These were in a much looser formation, with birds forming a long, scattered band several hundred yards long, frequently rising on thermals. These never descended to sea level. The largest flock, an estimated 300 birds, was circling at extreme height, eventually forming long straggling lines, somewhat like gulls flying to roost. Almost every flock was associated with a band of showers, in today's case mainly showers of hail. These fronts were regular throughout most of the day, moving in a south-westerly direction and interspersed with sunny periods. After every shower we witnessed a surge of skuas heading north, often at quite close range.

During the afternoon, the showers became heavier and more widespread, usually traversing Shetland's west coast, all the way south to Fitful Head, and if Foula was engulfed in black clouds simultaneously the skuas seemed to be moving in between there and the mainland. It was under these conditions that we saw the biggest numbers of the day. Very few flocks were seen flying through a shower. Interestingly, the only long-tailed skuas seen (a flock of three) were observed in the morning just before a shower, when they settled close offshore until it had passed.

Most groups of pomarine skuas passed by flying low over the sea, usually hugging wave troughs, always in straggling, almost single file formation with a bunch of birds at the front. A couple of flocks during sunny spells in the morning would circle upwards like soaring raptors, usually when close to land, for a couple of hundred feet before descending to sea level again as they drifted further offshore.

When we reached the car and looked back we saw another flock heading north, but we had had enough and could not physically manage any more. We were literally shaking from exhaustion and adrenalin. It took one hour to drive back home, even that was not easy due to sore backsides from eleven hours of sitting on rocks. Before going home, we stopped by at Martin's house. He asked, "So you reached the thousand?" Our reply goes without saying.

End of day totals were 2,053 pomarine, 21 Arctic and three long-tailed skuas, two Manx shearwaters and two great northern divers counted flying north. Springtime sea-watching rarely gets better than that. An epic day!

Editorial comment: *Although they are regularly seen from the Western Isles, like long-tailed skua the normal spring migration route of pomarine skua lies to the west of Shetland (e.g. Wynn et al. 2014), so unless weather conditions drive them within sight of land the number of records is small. Strong north-westerlies accompanied by squally showers during the last three weeks of May present an opportunity to see them. Over 100 were recorded during four years in the 1990s, but the numbers in 1992 were far greater than in any other year. On the same day as the record movement off Wats Ness described by Hugh and Mick, 147 were recorded passing Eshaness.*

The total population of pomarine skua is unknown, with an estimate of "several 10,000s of pairs" made by del Hoyo et al. (1996). Breeding success fluctuates in relation to numbers of lemmings, which are a staple food item. The remoteness of their breeding grounds makes them the least familiar of the northern hemisphere skuas, so their unpredictable appearances on migration – especially in spring – are exciting.

Boat trip to Out Skerries with Bobby Tulloch

12th May 1981
Nick Dymond

It was before the days of mobile phones, when I was RSPB warden in Fetlar. Bobby Tulloch, who lived in Mid Yell, got a message to me on 11th May via the Fetlar ferry, that next day he would pick me up in his boat around 8am at the Brough slipway on the west shore of Fetlar for a day-visit to Out Skerries. So he did, and we set off on the south-easterly trip to Skerries. When we reached the open sea it was quite rough and Bobby let me take the wheel to distract me from getting sea-sick, while he made the tea. We were more than half way when a conversation on the radio by two Whalsay men started, but Bobby, an expert on Shetland dialects, was struggling to understand them. Eventually he decided it was one Whalsay fishing boat skipper telling another Whalsay skipper where there were lots of fish, using an accentuated version of their dialect so that no other skippers could understand.

Approaching the islands Bobby took the wheel again and we were soon into the harbour and tying the boat up securely. We had a quick chat with Edwin and Marina Tait who live near the harbour. Edwin told us there were migrants all over the place, but unfortunately he had lots of machine knitwear work to get completed.

So Bobby and I set off to see what we could find. We tried to cover the village areas systematically, but with so many birds here, there and everywhere that proved to be impossible. The most numerous species were definitely wheatears and willow warblers, closely followed by fieldfares, but redstarts, whinchats and whitethroats were not far behind. Most amazing was our count of at least 30 bluethroats with some giving us fantastic close views. Four wrynecks were very nice and the one real rarity was a very smart male subalpine warbler [before recent taxonomic changes]. Other spring migrants in good numbers were tree pipits, pied flycatchers, lesser whitethroats, blackcaps, reed buntings, bramblings, swallows and house martins. Then there were a few spotted flycatchers, robins, sedge warblers, chaffinches, siskins and dunnocks, and lastly singles of icterine warbler, garden warbler, grasshopper warbler and song thrush and, amazingly, just one definite chiffchaff. We also saw one jackdaw, two whimbrels, and of course, quite a few rock pipits.

By late afternoon we decided to overnight in Skerries rather than set off to Fetlar, so I was able to stay with Edwin and Marina and Bobby slept on his boat. We departed to Fetlar early morning next day.

Our actual or estimated totals for all migrant species were as follows:

Table 1. Counts of migrants on Out Skerries, 12th May 1981.

OUT SKERRIES 12TH MAY 1981			
Sparrowhawk	1	Common whitethroat	c50
Sandwich tern	2	Icterine warbler	1
Common sandpiper	2	Blackcap	c12
Whimbrel	1	Garden warbler	1
Woodpigeon	2	Subalpine warbler	1
Wryneck	4+	Sedge warbler	8+
Song thrush	1	Grasshopper warbler	1
Fieldfare	c180	Willow warbler	c200
Bluethroat	30+	Chiffchaff	1
Redstart	c100	Swallow	c40
Whinchat	c120	House martin	c25
Wheatear	c200	White wagtail	2
Dunnock	2	Tree pipit	c80
Robin	3	Chaffinch	c10
Pied flycatcher	c40	Brambling	c20
Spotted flycatcher	5	Siskin	6
Lesser whitethroat	c12	Reed bunting	c35

Editorial comment: *In the mid-1990s the European breeding population of bluethroat was estimated at 545,126-1,376,505 pairs with an additional 100,000 pairs in Russia. By 2000 the estimate of the total European population was revised upwards to 4,500,000-7,800,000 pairs and considered stable, though there are few data from the rest of the global range* (Handbook of the Birds of the World).

In Shetland, numbers of migrants were high during the 1970s and 1980s but have decreased in recent decades. Clarke recorded a maximum of 12 in Fair Isle during 14-25th May 1910, then 60 were recorded in Fair Isle on 7-8th May 1936; the highest autumn count during the same period was 20 on 18th September 1931. After 1970 numbers increased, with over 80 per cent in spring. Notable spring influxes were recorded in 1970 (105+), 1981 and 1985 (both c220) and 1988 (c125). In 1985 there were 70 in Fair Isle on 13th May. Since then numbers have been lower, though 46 in 2019 was encouraging. The highest recent autumn total was 36 in 1988.

Evidence from Oland, Sweden, based on data between 1955 and 2008 (Svanbarg & Waldenstrom 2011), found that numbers have remained stable but median spring passage has become significantly earlier (13th May in 1999-2008, compared with 15th May or later during the two previous decades). Males precede females by about three days, and for most birds spring arrival into Sweden takes place within a short ten-day period in May.

Scops owl at Cunningsburgh

14th May 2001
Jim Nicolson

Since Shetland's landscape is practically treeless, about 15 years ago I acquired a small corner of land from a neighbouring crofter and began planting trees, mostly deciduous with a few conifers, hoping to attract the less common migratory birds as well as common visitors.

Monday 14th May started as usual. As a part-time worker, I did a couple of hours in the morning, returning home at 9.45am, with a light southerly wind and sunshine. I grabbed the binoculars and camera and headed for my small tree plantation near to my house at Cunningsburgh. As growth in Shetland is about a month behind mainland Britain, with only a few needles and leaves on the trees, I scanned the scene from a distance, seeing nothing unusual, only a few blackbirds, siskins and house sparrows. I moved in closer among the dozen or so conifers, none of them taller than twenty feet; Shetland being windswept limits their size. I was surprised to see a small owl no more than four feet from where I was standing, tucked in behind some branches. Knowing this was a very rare find, I moved back to a safe distance and to my amazement realised I had stumbled upon a scops owl. I quickly took a photo, raced back to the house and began to phone other birders on the 'Shetland grapevine'. The calls were brief, as most responded by just saying, "I'm on my way!" and laid the phone down. By 10.30 the first were arriving, with numbers building up by lunchtime. With this being only the eighth sighting in Shetland since 1900, and since birders from as far away as the outer isles of Unst, Yell and Fetlar (as well as a small plane load from Fair Isle) were coming to see the bird, it was decided to rope off a viewing area to prevent the bird from being flushed.

Many local villagers came to see the owl. Paul Harvey encouraged 'non-birders' to use his telescope so people could have a closer look, with the smaller children having to be lifted up. Not much bigger than a starling, many people commented on its small size.

All in all, around 60 people saw the owl before the last sighting as the light began to fade. The owl would soon leave its roost to hunt, which left us wondering if it would stay around for a few days but, as an insect-eater and insects being scarce in Shetland at this

Scops owl *(Otus scops)*, Cunningsburgh, May 2001, © Jim Nicolson.

time of year, it was not to be. Early morning checks over the next few days proved fruitless. The scops owl made Monday 14th May an exciting day, leaving Shetland birders eagerly awaiting the next rarity, wondering what it would be.

Editorial comment: *Martin & Mikkola (2019) discussed the northward expansion of scops owls into Scandinavia, following climate change, and suggested the possibility of future breeding in Scotland.*

Marmora's warbler at Baliasta, Unst

14th May 2018

David Cooper and Brenda Kay

After three days of what had felt promising south-easterly winds, whilst our garden had played host to a singing male bluethroat it's fair to say that the numbers and variety of grounded migrants had proved a little underwhelming. Overnight to the 14th May there had been a splash of rain, and perhaps just as importantly, a classic reversal in the wind direction to a north-westerly that sometimes seems to stop northbound spring migrants in their tracks.

An early morning visit to Skaw produced a lesser whitethroat and a willow warbler, so although there were still far more perches than birds, by this spring's standards it almost amounted to a fall. A walk along Lamba Ness added a female pied flycatcher sitting along a fenceline that added to my suspicion that there was a thin scatter of migrants grounded across the island. In fact, there then seemed something for every birder active in the island, with a succession of messages received relaying news of another pied flycatcher, a spotted flycatcher, a male red-backed shrike, a male bluethroat, a sedge warbler and a marsh warbler. As the migrants included some clearly bound for Scandinavia, I'd mentioned to Brenda the possibility that we might find a rustic bunting having found two spring birds in Unst in the last three years. Unbeknown to me, whilst leaving me to check a garden or two, Brenda had refreshed her memory of what to look for by taking a quick look in the Collins guide that was in our car.

We'd taken a long walk around Haroldswick and then visited Burrafirth but had seen very little. It was already mid-afternoon by the time we headed for Baltasound. Birders were present at all three of our first intended stops so we deviated from our planned route, but again saw very little at the sites that we checked. By late afternoon we decided to make the gardens along the road to Baliasta our last port of call for the day. We'd checked the gardens from the Manse to the cemetery that will be familiar to many birders as the area which the Cape May warbler frequented in the autumn of 2013. We were back in the car heading for Houlland when Brenda suggested that we take a look at a small sunken garden en route that looked something of a suntrap in the late afternoon sunshine. Having

Marmora's warbler *(Curruca sarda)*, Unst, May 2018, © David Cooper, "Oh, the all grey one with a red eye and orange bill and legs."

been out in the field for nearly 12 hours by then, I was flagging, and almost didn't bother to stop . . .

. . . I parked the car, and walked across the road to the dry stone wall opposite with the sun behind me. From immediately the other side of the wall, a tiny long-tailed *Sylvia* took flight, and with a typically weak and jerky flight it set off low across the rough grass towards the wall the other side of the c.30m-wide field. Its jizz was that of a Dartford warbler but its plumage appeared a uniform paler grey – even in that short flight – and the possibility of it being a Marmora's warbler flashed through my mind. It landed on the wall, perfectly lit by the sun, and basically appeared all slate-grey save for its darker lores, red eyes, pinkish base to its spiky bill and orange legs . . . and then it all too promptly hopped over the top of the wall and out of sight down the other side. Of all the miles of dry stone wall to walk up to, I'd literally had the good fortune to choose the correct square metre of wall!

Despite the whole encounter lasting just a few seconds, I shouted to Brenda that it was a Marmora's warbler, and for her to grab her camera. She rather calmly but reassuringly replied, "Oh, the all-grey one with a red eye and orange bill and legs." That rather took me by surprise, as she seemed to know as much about the species as there is to know. It transpired that whilst looking for buntings in the Collins guide, the *Sylvias* had caught her eye, especially Marmora's warbler, as it had an unfamiliar name that she'd never heard me mention until now.

I still don't recall how I sprang over the fence/wall combination and crossed half the field in pursuit, but as I cautiously crept the last few metres with camera poised, unbelievably there was no sign of it. I'd seen exactly where it had disappeared, and had remained transfixed, hopefully ensuring that I didn't miss it fly again. I rechecked along the wall but there was still no sign of it. As I looked up I could see walls stretching away into the distance in just about every direction. Surely we weren't to be left without any further views or images of it. Initially I was almost at a loss as to know where to look. The sunken garden itself had a few rosa rugosa bushes so I considered that the best place to start. I'd made my way halfway across the field towards them when, much to my relief, it flew right past me heading in the same direction. It landed on some bare earth and hopped, tail held half-cocked, into the depths below one of the bushes. Still no images, but it soon worked its way up through the bush and perched briefly on the adjacent wall allowing for more views and we both quickly rattled off some images. It disappeared over the wall and out of sight again. I checked my images, and whilst confirmatory, the camera settings weren't great being on a very high ISO.

We walked the wall, but again it had vanished in front of our eyes. We again checked the sunken garden and the immediate surrounding walls but there was no sign of it. Effectively we'd had two very brief encounters, but then completely lost it.

I explained to Brenda that Marmora's warbler had recently been split into two species, and that we needed to eliminate the, albeit unlikely, possibility of it being a Balearic warbler. Our first edition Collins guide pre-dated the split and I was struggling to recall the features of Balearic warbler. My own recollections of them from Mallorca were that they were paler, more silvery-grey in appearance compared to the only Marmora's warbler that I'd seen, the first-summer male at St Abbs in 1993 that I'd considered was darker, more sooty-grey in appearance. I'd already noted that ours was also showing some brownish hues to its upperparts, and particularly its wings, which I was fairly sure I could recall helped age the St Abbs bird as a first-summer.

With no mobile phone signal we drove to Houlland where we knew we would obtain a partial signal. It was already approaching 6pm, and I didn't think anyone would thank me for not putting the news out whilst we further considered the unlikely possibility of it being a Balearic warbler, so Brenda used her smartphone to transfer a couple of 'back of the camera' shots, along with an appropriate caveat that we didn't have any literature with us re Balearic warbler, onto the Shetland WhatsApp system. With the lack of bandwith available it took nearly ten minutes for each shot to upload to WhatsApp despite Brenda's arm being stuck up in the air out of the car window.

In the meantime I spoke to my father, John Cooper, and he very quickly checked the *Sylvias* Helm guide. The combination of its small white malar and dark throat swung it firmly in favour of Marmora's, although I could tell that he was slightly perplexed by me describing its underparts as showing some buff. I then phoned Brydon Thomason and pretty much just said, "Marmora's warbler, Baliasta, get here!" After a few expletives he said that he was about to take his son Casey to a youth club commitment but they'd now make their way via Baliasta. JFC then called me back to read me the text in the Helm guide relating to a first-summer Marmora's warblers that stated: "underparts more solidly coloured but, compared to adults, slightly duller and buffier overall". Hence, nothing at all seemed amiss for it being a Marmora's.

I then called Roger Riddington, whose initial reply was a simple, "Bloody hell!" I ran through the identification features that we were using and his words were something along the lines of: "It sounds like the job is done. I'd love to see it, please stick with it until 9pm as I should be there about then … " Whilst speaking to Roger the first WhatsApp message complete with photo pinged through. Paul Harvey soon phoned and ran through the features of Balearic and Marmora's warblers. Someone also took the trouble to send to Brenda's phone the complete Surfbirds article dealing with the identification of the two species written by Brian Small.

Of course, by now, we wanted to return to the site to try and relocate and watch the warbler and we simply didn't have time to reply to all of the incoming congratulatory messages. We returned and Brydon, Casey and Robbie Brookes were already there. Thankfully Brydon and Casey had obtained views of the warbler but it had done its, by now usual, vanishing act over the top of a wall. However, it didn't take long for it to reappear just prior to Al Conlin arriving. Brydon had helpfully brought his copy of *Sylvias;* seeing the plates only reinforced our view that it was a Marmora's and not a Balearic warbler. Whilst elusive, it seemed to have a discrete circuit feeding in and out of nooks in the dry stone walls. It helped that it was a lovely, sunny, warm and calm evening. Brydon and Casey left for the youth club beach clean-up, Brenda headed home and Al did likewise to tend to a chicken that he'd left cooking in his oven.

Robbie and I both decided that we would remain on site until 9pm but then we received the news that Mark Warren had found a black-faced bunting at Norwick. Dilemma; we decided that we just had enough time to take a look for, and hopefully see it, but still return to Baliasta before the birders arrived from the mainland. We failed to find the bunting but did arrive back at Baliasta, along with Brydon, just before Pete Ellis, Paul Harvey, Dougie Preston, Roger Riddington and Paul Sclater arrived off the ferry. A tense wait ensued, but just after the sun dropped below the hillside, the warbler obliged. It then gave its most prolonged and close views to the assembled small group of observers who in turn were giving a few "oohs" and "aahs" in appreciation. It gave a few quiet calls comprised of short, hard, slightly slurred and scolding "chak" notes strung together, that actually reminded me of a quiet version of some of the calls of a mobbing Arctic tern but very different from the long drawn-out churring call of a Dartford warbler. It also gave what two former members of BBRC considered was "a clear response" to a short playback of the song of Marmora's warbler: Brian Small's article suggested that neither species reacts to the playback of the other's song. It then flicked into a garden that offered plenty of suitable cover for it to roost and all the observers left the site.

The birders from Mainland were effectively stranded in Unst so a couple of them stayed at ours and the malt whisky flowed in celebration. I was so wired that I was still awake at 1am and it was proving a calm, clear and very bright night – unfortunately there was no sign of the Marmora's warbler or the black-faced bunting the next day.

Interestingly, the Marmora's warbler at Spurn in June 1992 also arrived amongst an east coast fall of birds of Scandinavian/northern European origin that included both red-backed shrike and marsh warbler (*Birding World* 5: 217).

The 1990 big bird race

Mick Mellor

When I crawled from my bed at 3.30am on 19th May 1990 for the annual sponsored bird race, I was not to know that it would turn out to be one of my most memorable birding days ever. One bird made this day very special indeed, but the overall quality of unusual species contributed to create an outstanding list at the end of the day.

The competition began when the other three team members (Martin Heubeck, Kevin Osborn and Dave Suddaby) picked me up from my home and we headed straight for Sumburgh Head, ticking off the first birds of the day as we drove south. Oystercatcher (1), fulmar (2), common gull (3), herring gull (4), lesser black-backed gull (5) and kestrel (6) all went down on paper before we arrived at the headland to settle down for about one hour of sea watching.

Everything seen here was normal run-of-the-mill stuff, but it boosted the list up to 21: kittiwake (7), gannet (8), shag (9), guillemot (10), razorbill (11), puffin (12), black guillemot (13), Arctic skua (14), rock dove (15), great skua (16), hooded crow (17), great black-backed gull (18), meadow pipit (19), wheatear (20) and wren (21).

The Grutness garden revealed a notable dearth of migrants, as did the Sumburgh Hotel garden, but the latter produced the inevitable starling (22) and house sparrow (23), along with twite (24) and blackbird (25). Overhead, skylarks (26) were singing while a couple of distant ravens (27) flew over Compass Head. The adjacent boggy fields gave us singing curlew (28), displaying lapwing (29) and drumming snipe (30), while singles of redshank (31) and rock pipit (32) were standing on the drystone dykes. More impressive was a great northern diver (33) in summer plumage floating close inshore in West Voe, a species we expected to see at some point later, but a good one to bag so early in the day. A brief scan over the rest of West Voe gave us long-tailed duck (34), eider (35) and common tern (36).

At Scatness we merely scanned from the road-end and managed to pick up a party of three wigeon (37) feeding at the edge of Loch of Gards, while the display song of ringed plover (38) was clearly audible in the distance. The Pool of Virkie could only offer us shelduck (39) and cormorant (40), so we drove north, calling at Heusbreck loch on the way – mallard (41) and common sandpiper (42), then pushed on towards Hillwell and the biggest surprise of the day.

Overlooking Hillwell Loch from the road we immediately picked up coot (43) and moorhen (44). Further scrutiny produced the only pintail (45) of the day (a female), a drake shoveler (46) and a long-staying drake garganey (47). A few swallows (48) and a pied wagtail (49) were also seen before we decided to walk along the burn that runs into the

Pallas's sandgrouse *(Syrrhaptes paradoxus)*, Quendale, May 1990, © Jack Levene.

loch. Someone had reported a wood sandpiper here very recently, that being our reason for walking the burn; however, this decision lost us three hours of the day but, believe me, I'm not complaining!

A bird flew low across our path and landed in a bare, sandy field about fifty yards away: almost lost for words we found ourselves looking at a Pallas's sandgrouse (50).

It was still well before six in the morning, but the news went out on the local grapevine, which in those days involved phoning several group leaders, who then had the responsibility of letting everyone else know. The distant sound of rapid gear changing and screeching tyres announced one of the first arrivals. However, the sandgrouse remained in the same field for most to see for quite some time, then took off and landed in a bigger field where it was harder to locate. Eventually it flew towards the east side of Quendale bay, giving us the cue to move on and try to make up for lost time. Totally amazing. What an incredible find!

Incidentally, the wood sandpiper (51) did appear during the time we spent at Hillwell. Afterwards, while driving around Loch of Spiggie we found some of the more expected birds such as Arctic tern (52), black-headed gull (53), tufted duck (54), red-breasted merganser (55), red-throated diver (56) and a couple of whooper swans (57), while bonus birds consisted of goldeneye (58), a drake scaup (59) and a greenshank (60).

By this stage, we had the bulk of the common species ticked off, so with renewed inspiration we still thought we had a chance to win the competition, even though our rivals had gained two hours on us. At Geosetter burn we saw the only robin (61) of the day, while Bigton produced blackcap (62) and an unexpected common redstart (63).

Having done the Ness, we headed north to Lerwick, where the trees at Helendale revealed wood pigeon (64), collared dove (65), chaffinch (66) and lesser whitethroat (67). The rocky shoreline along Seafield Road produced singles of turnstone (68) and grey heron (69), but no sign of the hoped-for purple sandpiper, this being the only locality where we saw them the previous year.

After very welcome breakfast at the P&O ferry terminal we drove over to the Gremista Industrial Estate and picked up a single Iceland gull (70) in a field and a glaucous gull (71) on the fish factory roof. How lucky can you get.

Onwards to Scalloway where the song of a chiffchaff (72) gave itself up in one of the larger gardens, while the second lesser whitethroat of the day was also heard singing. We continued north, picking up reed bunting (73) in the Tingwall Valley. Continuing further north, we stopped beside the large Sandwater Loch, where an osprey had been reported on a regular basis recently. After what seemed like only a matter of seconds, there it was! Osprey (74) standing on a rock, half-way up a hillside at the opposite side of the loch. It soon lost patience with a couple of hooded crows, so it took off and began circling over the loch, gradually gaining height. This happened to be the first osprey I had seen in Shetland.

Not many miles away a desperate stomp across endless heather moorland produced breeding whimbrel (75) and golden plover (76) before we pushed on to Catfirth, where a random search of a conifer plantation gave us a surprise long-eared owl (77). A similar looking conifer stand at South Nesting produced a couple of song thrush (78), but at Vidlin we had to work hard before finding the two long-staying bee-eaters (79) as they were not in their favoured garden. However, we eventually located them from their distinctive calls feeding over nearby grass pastures.

A merlin (80) was seen in Northmavine as we belted north to Eshaness to look for another long-staying rare bird: common crane (81). We saw one of a party of three birds which had been in the area for a couple of weeks, in fact there could still have been three, but we ticked off the first one and continued driving north. A totally unexpected bonus was a turtle dove (82) which flew across in front of the car and perched conveniently on some telephone wires. It certainly looked out of place in the barren, treeless Eshaness landscape.

At our next destination we started scanning the high rock face at the foot of Ronas Hill. After several minutes one team member's keen eye picked out the bird we were hoping for, a very distant peregrine (83) sitting near the top of the cliffs, its black hood and pale underparts clinching the identification beyond any doubt.

Heading south again we picked up teal (84) from an unnamed weedy loch somewhere in North Mainland, then we found a redwing (85) in the trees at Voe; this bird was behaving very elusively and was certainly among good breeding habitat.

Continuing south I spotted a dunlin (86) at Sandwater Loch – because I had missed one earlier in the day, this meant that we could now officially add it to the list. We then drove to Kergord. About one hour was spent scouring the trees where we expected to add just a couple of species. To our surprise we succeeded in adding a further six. Apart from the expected rook (87) and goldcrest (88), we also saw cuckoo (89), tree pipit (90), brambling (91) and pied flycatcher (92). The last four species were all bonus birds and certainly an important boost to the day's tally.

We still had several hours of daylight left, and just two species short of the previous year's total we headed out to West Mainland and almost immediately picked up the residing drake king eider (93), swimming in the middle of Tresta Voe with a few of its commoner relatives.

While driving back through Lerwick we made one more attempt for purple sandpiper

(94) and were lucky. Just one bird standing on rocks at Seafield was all that we needed to bring us level with the previous year's grand total.

With at least four hours of daylight left we only managed to add one more species. A long time was devoted to yomping moorland for red grouse, but to no avail. The final addition to an extraordinary day list came in the form of the humble house martin (95), with five over Spiggie loch at dusk.

The scarcity of common migrants (neither team saw, or heard, a willow warbler) did not detract from an amazing day's birding, and surprisingly we even won the competition. Of course, we were in high spirits as we ended the day at the Sumburgh Hotel celebrating our big find with several hard-core listers who had already flown up to Shetland and 'twitched' the sandgrouse.

Editorial comment: *An account of Shetland's first Pallas's sandgrouse was given by Saxby (1874). On 28th October, 1863, he saw a bird which* "puzzled me a great deal"; *initially the whirring sound of its wings and buffy colour attracted attention, and was enough for Saxby to suggest a provisional identification following reports from England and Scotland. He saw it again briefly the following day, and again heard the sound of its wings and* "four short single notes, very unlike those of any bird with which I am acquainted". *It was not until 2nd November that he saw it again, this time well enough to confirm that it was a sandgrouse. The bird was shy and flighty, but Saxby noted:* "a pale buffy colour, and even at great distance a black patch was very conspicuous. As it flies it frequently utters a succession of short notes sounding something like the words 'tiou, tiou, tiou'. The bird while flying has a good deal the appearance of a Golden Plover, but its flight is even more rapid". *Finally, on 4th November, its habit of returning to a turnip crop proved its undoing and Saxby shot it:* "He is, as I supposed, a specimen of Pallas' Sand Grouse (*Syrrhaptes paradoxus*). The latter name is well bestowed, for a more puzzling bird I never saw."

1863 was the year of the first recorded major influx in Britain (Slack 2009), and was followed by an influx of over 5,000 – and several breeding records – in 1888, possibly in response to heavy snowfall making it difficult to survive in the normal breeding areas. Forty reached Fair Isle in early June 1888. Since 1969 there have been just two records: two on the Isle of May on 11th May 1975, and the 1990 Shetland bird which was present from 19th May until 4th June. Whether the comment, "That pigeon looks like a sandgrouse!" will be made again is a good question, given the combined effects of loss of breeding habitat and climate change.

Fair Isle

23rd May 2012
Kevin Kelly

There is something truly special about island birding: finding yourself trying to select the perfect week, long before travel, and nervously watching the weather reports and bird sightings inevitably consume one's attention in the weeks preceding a trip. I now live and work in Shetland, so am fortunate that the headache and feeling of rolling the dice has subsided somewhat when migration season arrives.

I would certainly say I am a migration addict, blown away year on year by this incredible natural phenomenon. Although now living amongst the spectacle, it is an annual trip to Fair Isle – which reduces the area to cover each day – that lures me in. Nothing beats the thrill of heading out each day and observing the changes and movements that occur.

A week in Fair Isle in the second half of May is always exciting, but when the weather also aligns the outcome is long days in the field with plenty of birds, often in their summer finery too. I could have regaled many great days that consisted of superb rarities, huge autumn arrivals or personal finds. However, the week that still consistently makes me smile when reflecting back is a week of truly perfect spring birding, that had included some memorable birds (albeit nothing classed as rare).

This specific week in 2012 boasted clear skies, warm days and light easterly winds intermittently throughout the week, making perfect conditions for seeing drift and overshoot migrating birds heading north.

The week had an almost constant run of headline species – thrush nightingale, hoopoe, common nightingale, red-rumped swallow, shorelark, short-toed lark, bluethroats, red-backed shrikes, wrynecks and icterine warblers amongst others – and the consistent turnover of new birds made the entire week highly enjoyable. One day in the week stands out from the rest for me, not because of anything scarce or rare particularly on that day, but more because of the quality and quantity of the species in their summer attire that made landfall.

Wednesday 23rd May was my last full day birding in Fair Isle and again the weather was excellent: light easterlies and warm, clear skies. As had been the theme for the week, I was awake and out by 5am for a pre-breakfast foray into the field to search for newly arrived migrants. The early signs were promising as it soon became apparent that there was an arrival of birds and it seemed like every suitable spot held a different bird compared to the previous day.

Red-rumped swallow *(Cecropis daurica)*, Fair Isle, May 2012, © Kevin Kelly.

Red-backed shrike *(Lanius collurio)*, Fair Isle, May 2012, © Kevin Kelly.

One of the joys of spring birding is that, even on quiet days, the numbers of breeding seabirds make for very enjoyable birding, with Arctic and great skuas harassing Arctic terns, and puffins and other auks busily whipping in and out of the cliff tops.

After enjoying a leisurely start, watching the aerial acrobatics of an Arctic skua, and a stunning knot in its summer plumage prodding through the seaweed, I set off ambling my way north, which I had decided was to be the plan for the day; but first I would carry out a circuit of the fields and crofts in the south before breakfast. I set off eagerly checking the accessible croft gardens en route, and the list of common migrants was superb, with a new bird added to the day list at almost every croft garden.

A quick check of Utra revealed that a wryneck was still present, briefly alighting on the wall before vanishing down the opposite side. The garden at Auld Haa was next on my search, with a truly stunning male common rosefinch that I had found a few days earlier still on the feeders here, whilst chiffchaffs and blackcaps flitted around the bushes and a willow warbler blasted out a hopeful song. The crofts at Burkle and Quoy added garden warbler, lesser and common whitethroat and spotted flycatcher to the day's tally, and three tree pipits perched on the fence too.

Crossing over the road to Schoolton a zesty icterine warbler paused in the same rosa as a female type common rosefinch, and another spotted flycatcher was in close attendance. The heat of the day was already being felt and the birds on my journey north would continue to impress; redstarts, lesser whitethroats and blackcaps were numerous, but they were certainly outstaged in numbers by spotted flycatchers whose numbers increased by early afternoon.

Seeing a species arrive in large numbers is one of the biggest thrills of migration for me, and the fenceline from the back of Chalet down to Pund was a resounding example of this, with 12 spotted flycatchers dotted around the fences and a shot of colour thrown into the middle in the form of a striking whinchat. The walk onwards to Plantation was a visual feast, with yet more common migrants en route. Pausing on arrival at Plantation I opted to sit and observe the vegetated entrance to the Heligoland trap. The first bird to reveal itself was a male red-backed shrike, catching bees and insects around the trap area, quickly joined by a second, with another found feeding along the fence posts too, making the area feel like a typical summer's day in eastern Europe.

Arriving up at the bird observatory garden it was clear that red-backed shrikes had increased on the previous day, with another couple buzzing around the garden. A little stake out at the garden area gave a truly unforgettable visual for the next hour. A different species each time would parade itself along the sunny edge of the trees, before making way for the next. The stunning conveyer belt of birds consisted of the following totals: four icterine warblers (all in view at once), three lesser whitethroats, four willow warblers, two chiffchaffs, two blackcaps, one sedge warbler, one pied flycatcher, two spotted flycatchers, two redstarts, two tree pipits and two red-backed shrikes (both males). Migration at its best, with a beautiful collection of birds feeding up for their onward journey. Overhead came the excited 'zip' of swallows as a group of six with a house martin for company made their way out to South Haven.

The total haul for the day of some species was truly unforgettable, with red-backed shrikes totalling nine at log that night, seven of which were very smart males; they were topped only by the incredible 10 icterine warblers though, of which I managed to see eight throughout the day including a couple of singing individuals too. A good selection were trapped and ringed in the early evening and throughout the day, including icterine warblers and a few of the red-backed shrikes.

The unexpected highlight of the day above the scarcities, however, was the arrival of spotted flycatchers; almost every fence line, rock or dyke seemingly had one. The number logged that night was 64, but it certainly felt like more!

A visit to see two smart dotterel on my journey back south rounded off the day and almost concluded the excellent week of migration.

After sadly bidding farewell to Fair Isle and arriving back in South Mainland, the week had one last treat in store. The following day I had been searching for migrants around the stone dykes at RSPB Sumburgh Head and the surrounding fields, when an unfamiliar song trilled out. I quickly searched the archive of my mind to match the song, but it was not familiar. Its source soon revealed itself on the top of the wall: a stunning male rustic bunting. It foraged in the area while I put news out and headed off back to the hotel preparing to say goodbye to another special week of migration in Shetland.

There have been many special days since, but that spring week and, in particular, that day will always make me smile. Classic Shetland.

Foula

2nd June 2019
Paul Bloomer

I was in Foula on a 'curry club' visit which is usually in September to coincide with autumn migration, but someone suggested an extra curry club visit in late May. Curry club is an excuse for some long-term friends to get together regularly with the common theme of eating curry and drinking beer in good company.

A few very keen birders are part of the group and birding is embedded into these Foula visits. A scour of the island revealed very few migrants, a few common warblers with a beautiful subalpine warbler at Ham garden and the by now semi-tame 'yellow-legged gull' residing on the roof of Geoff and Donna's house. Saturday night in Foula is usually a 'tunes' night when the locals get together and the music flows into the morning. I decided to bail out of the music at about 12.30am as I was keen to go out early next day to look for a white-tailed eagle that was last seen disappearing over the Noup a few days earlier by Geoff.

Very heavy rain fell overnight and was still falling and this, coupled with the post-tunes tiredness of the house as well as general lack of migrants, meant there was no rush to get out at all. Most of the house decided to sleep in apart from Howard Towll who was out early to draw bonxies. The traditional curry club breakfast is whisky porridge, which went down well, followed by a few rum coffees to take the edge off the lashing rain as well as give a false sense of courage to go out and explore Foula. As my sights were set on going round and up the Noup to drop down at the Sneck of the Smaalie I decided to stay on the road instead of the usual route down the Ham burn.

The rain was relentless, my waterproofs were starting to seep and I was getting wetter and wetter. I stopped off to check Ham garden where there was a garden warbler and chiffchaff, then marched on, not really in a birding groove. I started to climb up and round the Noup but quickly found myself at cloud level with visibility extremely limited. I decided to abandon the idea of going higher and made my way into the valley that leads to the Sneck. Here, the ground was so waterlogged it was over the top of my walking boots, so I also abandoned that plan and made my way back to the road. I checked a few of the gardens and slowly went back to Ham where the plan was to eat food and drink hot tea from my flask. The subalpine warbler showed itself and the burn was now alive with house

Little bittern, image from an original painting by Paul Bloomer.

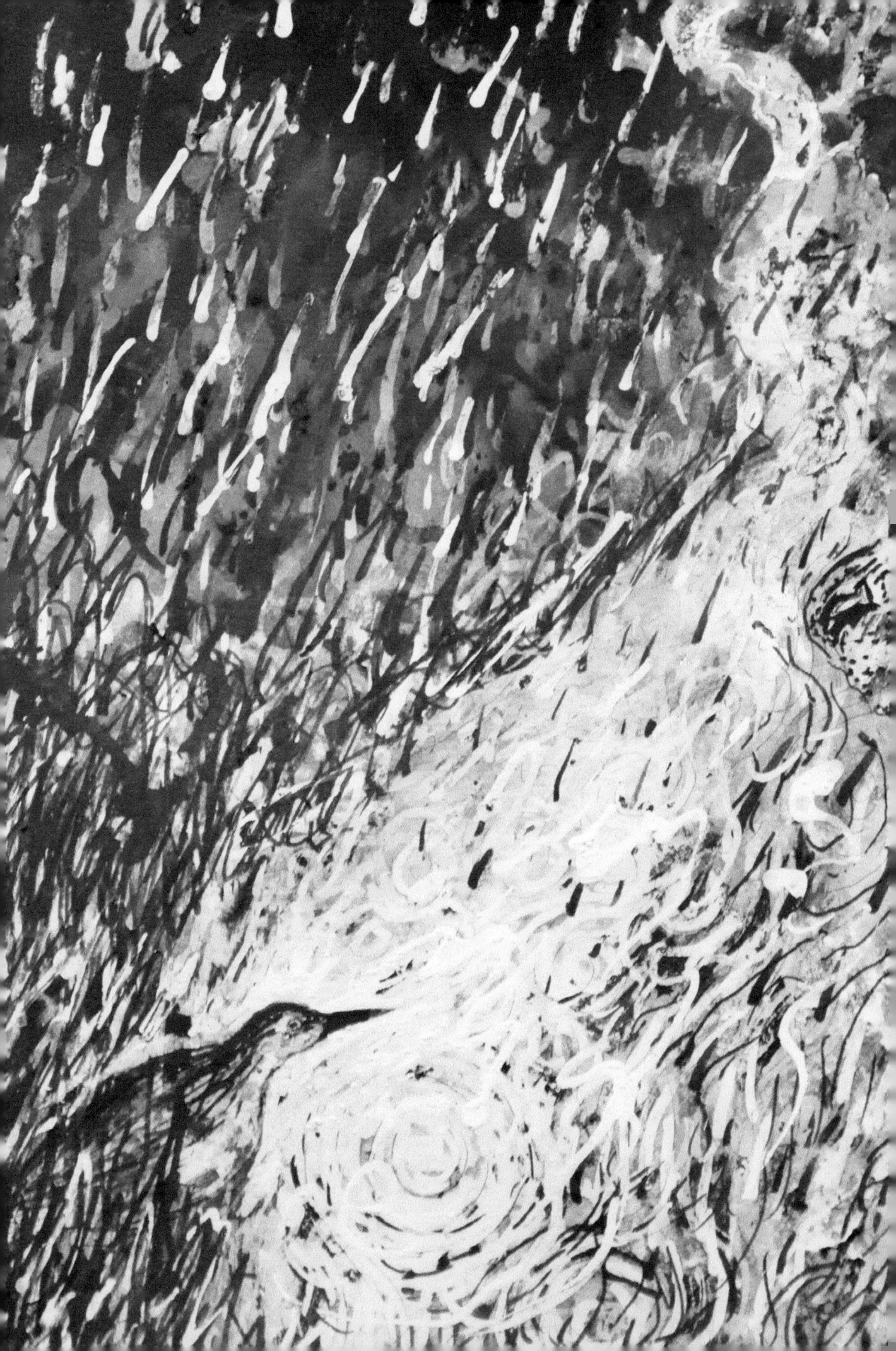

Little bittern *(Ixobrychus minutus)*, Foula, June 2019, © Paul Bloomer, "A beautiful golden yellow bird with trailing yellow legs."

martins and swallows which I really enjoyed spending time with.

My plan was to fly fish the Mill Loch for trout with the telescopic rod I keep in my bag, but something told me not to, this instinctive voice somewhere deep within that I try my hardest to trust. Slightly buoyed up but still soaking wet I started the trek back to Ristie, and when I got to Burns I decided to cut inland to follow the Ham burn back up. One chiffchaff and a few house martins showed there were at least a few migrants about, but nothing to make me really want to focus too hard on looking for rare birds. I was increasingly being drawn in by the patterns on the land created by the multitude of small water flows that were flowing into the main burn. Near the bend where there is a large pool of water I started to look a bit more closely for a sedge warbler that was present the day before. I noticed at my feet a small brown trout lying dead on the bank, which I thought a strange thing to see and, as I thought about possible reasons this fish might be there, a beautiful golden-yellow bird with trailing yellow legs lifted from slightly upstream and flew straight past me then landed nearby.

Luckily I had a camera and got a few photos before it slinked into the heather then flew downstream towards Ham. This magical, golden mini-heron was tiny, and I checked the photo against the Collins bird app on my phone to realise it was a little bittern. There was no phone reception where I was so it was a wee while before I could send a message to the rest of the curry club, some of whom I knew would be keen to see it. I wanted a second opinion on the identification so I put the photo on the general BaltiBoyz WhatsApp where I knew a few heavyweight birders/curry eaters such as Paul Harvey and Will Miles would see it (though neither could make it into Foula). First to chirp up was Rory Tallack who thought it was a wind-up, before realising I wasn't spinning a yarn and confirming its identity as a little bittern.

I needed to get a message to Geoff and Donna Atherton to give them the chance of seeing it, so although I had been on my feet for about eight hours already and was soaking wet I made my way back to Ham. Geoff nearly choked on his beans on toast when I told them there was a little bittern in the burn, and they were out like a flash leaving me unable to keep up. Our plan was to walk back up the burn whilst Juan Brown, who had by now recovered from the tunes-night refreshments, walked down towards us.

Not far from my original sighting it lifted again, veering off to the right slightly before disappearing out of sight in the heather and drainage ditches. Donna, Juan and Geoff got a look at the bird but despite scouring the area it had disappeared from view.

A text from Paul Harvey, who was due to be in Foula with us but pulled out at the last minute, gave a picture of the rarity of this bird: first for Foula, sixth for Shetland with the last two being in 1997 and 1965.

I wouldn't describe myself as a serious 'birder', but the reality is that birds have been the focus of my life since childhood and provide much inspiration for my art. I wasn't consciously or actively looking for a rare bird on this occasion and was more interested in the patterns of flow of the flood water and enjoying the whole scene around me, so this bird was the last thing I was expecting to see. If there is a lesson, I would say try not to be driven by the sometimes desperate quest for rarities as this can blind us from enjoying the bigger, beautiful, natural world around us. Another lesson is to actually go outside and look rather than lie in bed all day, which was tempting to do on such an uncomfortable day. Even on days that seem to be very unpromising gold can still fall from the sky.

Noss

8th June 1998
Juan Brown

It was a visit to Noss in July 1994 that ultimately sealed my fate, and resulted in me living in Shetland 27 years on. After a thwarted attempt to visit the island on the Monday during a week in Shetland (Noss is closed on Mondays and Thursdays!), we returned the next day, when the Zodiac ferry was plying the turquoise waters of Noss Sound. After the obligatory introductory talk, we made our way across the low ground towards the cliffs, past Hill Dyke where Shetland wrens belt out their song, and along the coast to Cradle Holm, where the puffins are so tame they'll pull at your shoelaces. Just beyond Cradle Holm is Noss's *pièce de résistance,* the point when the mighty Noup cliff suddenly looms into view, the thousands of gannets on the cliff and in the air an assault on at least three senses. But we had to carry on a little further for our quarry.

Although the lingering Alpine swift was the reason for our visit, it ended up playing second fiddle to the Noup backdrop, as it snapped at the midges around our heads while we rested at the clifftop.

That visit to Noss had made an impression on me and three years later inspired me to write a speculative letter to Paul Harvey (who was managing the island at the time and who I'd met that day) from a posting on the Farnes, to see if there was a warden's job going. There was, and following a hasty 'interview' (involving meeting Jonathan Swale in a pub in York), Andy Upton, my Farnes co-conspirator, and I found ourselves in Shetland in April 1998 for the start of the Noss season. Despite being lashed by northerly gales for much of the 1998 summer, life in Noss was the idyll I had anticipated, and we were straight into the birding. A goldfinch in the garden (first for Noss) and wryneck above the cliffs at Charlie's Holm, plus a steady trickle of common and 'scarce-for-Noss' migrants, got things off to a good start, and fired us up for the rest of our time on the island.

Noss suited my birding down to a tee, being a plodding patcher as opposed to a manic racer. It takes three hours to walk around Noss's perimeter, so you have to pace yourself. My philosophy was to go for a walk around the island, and bumping into a goodie was a bonus. This avoided the inevitable burn-out that comes quickly when heightened expectancy is met by a total lack of migrant birds (which, after all, is the norm). The reason why Noss suited this 'tortoise' approach for me is that every time I set off on the hike around the island it felt like an expedition, and I would never be disappointed by the spectacle of the Noup and its throng of gannets, the clusters of guillemots in the honeycombed cliffs

Noss, looking towards the Noup, © Juan Brown, "I would never be disappointed by the spectacle of the Noup and its throng of gannets."

of Cradle Holm, or an encounter with puffins. Anything else was a bonus. So it kept me coming back for more.

This approach to birding was subsequently epitomised for me during a stint on Skomer by the 'king of plodders', Mike Pilsworth (who coincidentally was with me on that first visit to Noss), who had an astounding strike-rate one autumn, simply by being exceptionally laid-back, but continuing to plod on. I could only follow in his slipstream.

And Noss birds would come out of the blue. No waiting for easterly gales, driving rain and 'falls'. A glimpse of a gaudy male western subalpine warbler appearing for a few seconds from the cliff dyke, before 'melting' back into same dyke, on a sunny day in June; the Bonelli's warbler that appeared on the garden fence in a westerly gale; and the spring olive-backed pipit foraging on the North Croo terraces; all arriving without supporting cast.

But the 'birding day' I will pick for this account has all the key elements that encapsulate my time on Noss; namely drunken caper aftermath, aborted seabird monitoring, and the element of surprise with a top-drawer rarity in a spectacular location.

Sunday, 7th June 1998, must have been a heavy night, with Steve Votier (a PhD student at the time, with Noss as one of his study sites) and I waking up on Monday morning at Islesburgh Hostel. After breakfast at the Harbour Cafe, we made our way back to Noss where we found Andy, having billeted in his car on Bressay. Although Monday was supposed to be our day off, lousy weather had set back seabird monitoring, so I followed Andy to the cliffs once I had said farewell to Steve, who was heading back to Hermaness (one of his other study sites).

I initially headed for my kittiwake plot at Heogatoug, but a brisk north-westerly wind soon put paid to any hope of collecting any data there. I decided to head for the Hangcliff gannets, via Andy who was hunkering down at the viewpoint to South Noup. After some brief words with Andy, I continued down along the low stone dyke bordering the cliff edge. Before I reached the corner at Rumblewick, a dumpy passerine with a stripy head popped up on the wall. Initial thoughts of rustic bunting were soon dispelled; the bird had a sulphur-yellow fore-supercilium, and was clearly a white-throated sparrow!

I screamed at Andy over the hand-held radio and he was with me in a flash, but the bird just seemed to have melted back into the wall and we couldn't relocate it. By this time Steve should have been well on his way to Hermaness, but as he had a reputation for stretching the weekends out on his visits south I knew there was just a chance he could still be around, despite no signs of life from the radio base station at Gungstie. I looked across to the Noss car park on Bressay and, sure enough, his red car was still there.

I called the Gungstie base set with increasing urgency, keen to catch Steve before he left the island. Finally, a response. Meanwhile, Andy had relocated the bird. It showed for ten minutes before doing its disappearing act again, and Steve took an hour of searching before he finally connected.

Paul Harvey had heard the commotion over the airwaves from his desk at the SNH office in Lerwick and a twitching party consisting of himself, Roger Riddington, Paul Goddard, Kevin Osborn and John and Dennis Coutts made it over that evening, marching up the hill in an ever lengthening line, the fitter members of the pack striding out front. Of course the bird had decided to give itself up by then, and they were treated to crippling views as it hopped, dunnock-like, on the coastal sward, long tail slightly cocked.

Once everyone had left, I returned to the bird to get some notes for a description and we spent the last hour of the day together. It seemed to be more active, and was starting to call (a sharp *speest*). The next day it had gone.

Now, over a quarter of a century later, I see Noss every day, having settled in Sandwick. Although I am privileged to be involved in managing the island again (and have seen some quality birds on there in the intervening years), nothing will compare to living in the island; a very special place indeed.

Birding the oil boom years

1975-1985

Ray O'Reilly

It was on Saturday, 21st June 1975, when I first set foot in Shetland as a 17-year-old lad, arriving on the *St Clair* in Lerwick during P&O Ferries' inaugural year of running the service. I made my way up to Unst by bus, seeing my first ever adult male red-breasted flycatcher at Halligarth, and onto Hermaness for Albert Ross, as it was called by then. The black-browed albatross didn't disappoint as I watched it interacting with gannets and soaring above the cliffs in a fulmar-like fashion.

The next day I caught the ferry over to Fetlar to see the breeding snowy owls; mainly around Vord Hill, they would occasionally come lower and on one occasion I could see the bird from the phone box in Houbie. During this time I phoned my friend Dick Filby (later of Rare Bird Alert fame) in Surrey and described the scene to him: the envy on the other end of the line was palpable.

I spent the following fortnight enjoying the breeding birds of Shetland and also the history and scenery of the islands and it was love at first sight. Over the following eight years I had a plethora of jobs in both the fishing and the oil industry, working mainly around Sullom Voe and Toft but also at Sumburgh, Lerwick, Bressay and Fair Isle.

Other English birders that I knew who also came up to the islands from that time on were Mark Chapman, Clive Byers, Franko Mareovic, Barry Walker, Rodney Martins, Billy Fletcher, Jim Hall, Greg Bashford and Craig Robson. We soon made friends with the Shetland birders of the time including Dennis Coutts, Bobby Tulloch, Dave Okill and a very young Andrew Graham.

One of the best finds during the decade was a dusky thrush at Firth on 6th November 1975. Barry Walker and a friend decided to go to Lerwick on their day off and they walked down to the main road from Toft Camp to hitch a lift into Lerwick. Barry told me from his home in Peru: "It was a cold, frosty morning and a fair number of fieldfares were hopping around near the roadside. I noticed that one of them was different so I got my bins out of my pack and was sure that it was a dusky thrush. I double-checked the field guide and started making phone calls." He went on to say,"It was quite a find as I wasn't even actively birding." The bird stayed until 13th November in sparse habitat and was photographed.

I received a phone call from Billy Fletcher in Fair Isle on the evening of 25th May 1976 to say that he had seen a funny kestrel that had been seen to go to roost. The following morning it had been confirmed as an adult male American kestrel which stayed until the following day, showing quite well on occasions. Billy sketched and painted the bird. I was in England and travelled down to Cornwall for the second record a couple of weeks later, this bird being a female on Bodmin Moor, suggesting that both birds' provenance was sound.

During our time working in Shetland we lived off camp in many locations and one such location was the school yard at Gott, opposite Strand Loch, the home of Andrew Graham's parents, Lollie and Mary. We would often work Strand Plantation and Veensgarth between us. The latter site in those days held a long-eared owl roost of up to ten birds and, on 17th June 1976, I had a singing male ortolan bunting. Other notable species at the former site were great reed warbler on 10th June 1976 and on 2nd June 1978 a male black-headed bunting; both of those birds were also singing.

It wasn't unusual for us to fly over to Fair Isle for a rare bird but on 12th September 1976 we flew from Fair Isle back to Sumburgh to see Shetland's first stilt sandpiper; it was only the second Scottish record and just the 11th for the UK. Amazingly, one of our group had seen one on a YOC (Young Ornithologists Club) trip to Minsmere, Suffolk, a couple of years previously. This bird was on the Loch of Gards, Scatness. This was also the site of my only personal addition to the Shetland list. My parents moved to Shetland in April 1977 and I would often stay with them at Hestingott. On 8th September 1979 I went birding to Scatness from their home and noticed a pair of ducks in eclipse or juvenile plumage that reminded me of odd garganey: their bills looked heavy, shoveler-like, and I thought they were blue-winged teals, but I waited until they left the water and stood upon rocks, clearly showing their yellow legs and feet, before I put the news out (garganey have dark legs and feet).

Many of the birds mentioned in this piece are not so rare today but in those days they were 'megas'. For instance, Jim Hall and I were working a cabbage crop at Kenaby in Fair Isle on 20th September 1976 when we flushed a chunky looking *Locustella* warbler; thinking that it was likely a Pallas's grasshopper warbler we contacted Roger Broad, the Observatory warden, and he soon had the bird in the hand showing us its white tail-spots. This was the first UK record for 20 years!

A red letter day was 13th August 1977 when I was having lunch in the Queen's Hotel, Lerwick. Rodney Martins walked through the door with a deadpan expression and proclaimed, "Guess which first for Britain I have just found?" We were straight in a taxi and arrived at the now famous Boddam garden watching a male Ruppell's warbler in next to no time. We worked the Ness until dusk that day adding spotted redshank and two wood sandpipers.

Talking of firsts for Britain, on 13th October 1980 we flew to Fair Isle to see a male yellow-browed bunting at Setter that at the time was regarded as a first, but a Norfolk record was subsequently accepted from 1975, making it the second. It remains an exceptionally rare bird. On that day in the island, I saw several house x tree sparrow hybrids, something that I have never observed elsewhere during a lifetime of birding. A common feature of inter-island travel by air was delays due to weather and we would often spend many fraught hours sitting around Sumburgh Airport. At that time Loganair would issue canteen vouchers and we would join the line of oil workers to obtain hot food and tea and coffee.

On 4th November 1977 I travelled up to Yell to see an adult rose-coloured starling. I

Black-throated thrush *(Turdus atrogularis)* or hybrid, Ward of Scousburgh, October 2019, © Ray O'Reilly.

can visualise it now riding around on the backs of Shetland sheep, another sight that I have never managed elsewhere.

I travelled down to Quendale on 6th November 1977 to see the third Shetland record of black-throated thrush as it fed in a field overlooking the Loch of Hillwell; little did I know that day that 42 years later I would find another one, this time on the Ward of Scousburgh (although it is thought by some that that bird may have had dusky thrush genes also). When time allowed we would attend the Shetland Bird Club meetings and in late December 1977 a freshly dead Brunnich's guillemot was passed around the room for inspection.

On 28th April 1978 we had made another journey to Fair Isle to see Britain's second and Shetland's first calandra lark at Field. The bird gave a couple of display flights, enhancing our enjoyment of it. We worked the whole of the south end of the island that day not seeing another migrant bird. Encouragement for those quieter days.

I caught the Whalsay ferry on 18th May 1979 hoping for the reported white-billed diver and wasn't disappointed; the bird surfaced at the side of the vessel and showed itself to be in mostly breeding plumage with a yellow bill. As a bonus a superb adult pomarine skua appeared in the vessel's wake showing a full spoon-shaped tail.

On 23rd May 1979 we made the short crossing to Bressay and were soon watching a spanking adult male collared flycatcher, and this time on working the island after the sighting we were luckier, being rewarded with a fine short-toed lark.

A total surprise for us was on 10th June 1979 when birding in a group that contained Mark Chapman and Greg Bashford at Sumburgh Farm. The song sparrow, that we had flown over to Fair Isle some two months previously to see, appeared in front of us. We knew that it was the same bird as it was ringed but it hadn't been seen on Fair Isle for over a month. Could this bird really have been around Sumburgh all that time without anyone seeing it, as it was fairly confiding?

It was 25th October 1980 when I had a call from my friend, the helicopter pilot and birder Ivan Davidson, who told me that he had a Swainson's thrush in his garden at Scatness. The bird favoured a compost heap and was another first for Shetland and only the sixth British record.

Clive Byers, Mark Chapman and Craig Robson told me a tale that during the spring of 1981 they were looking at the shoreline of the Sumburgh side of Quendale Bay, when a pipit in smart breeding plumage popped up in front of them. "It was unstreaked and rosy-buff below and had a large supercillium of a similar colour." They were all familiar with summer water pipits and Scandinavian rock pipits and identified the bird as an American water pipit (then a race, but today known as buff-bellied pipit). The bird appeared in the 1981 Shetland Bird Report but was rejected by the BBRC (British Birds Rarities Committee). Clive made a painting of the bird. That same year there was a long-staying drake green-winged teal at Sand Water and Strand Loch which we would often see from the minibus on the way home or to work between 14th March and 4th April.

Mark Chapman was the sole observer of a small crake that he saw running through the grassy dunes at West Voe, Sumburgh on 9th November 1982. He flushed the bird and identified it as an adult Baillon's crake. It was published in the Shetland Bird Report for that year but once again not accepted by the BBRC.

Clive tells another interesting tale of when he was birding at Fladdabister on 18th May 1983 and heard a bluethroat singing from the inside of a planticrub. He crept up and peered over the edge of the wall and the bird was singing from inside a lobster creel of which the twine matched the bird's throat colour exactly!

A phone call from Dave Okill to Clive Byers early on 13th September 1983 stating that the reported hawk owl was present at Frakkafield meant he had to drive with Barry Walker to site with a fast-beating heart; the bird had moved slightly and was sitting in a dead tree in the garden of a ruined croft house halfway up the hill. It was preening and looking very alert when suddenly it spiralled up in the sky in an *Accipiter*-like fashion and headed off towards Gremista. Franko Maroevic had arrived off the ferry that morning and missed the bird by half an hour or so and never saw it.

On 10th October 1985 Clive Byers, Mark Chapman and Andrew Graham were birding around Catfirth, checking out some of the gardens. Unlike a decade previously when yellow-browed warblers were fairly scarce in Shetland, this day there were plenty. The day had a feel of something in the air and as they were walking up the drive to look into a garden they flushed a large thrush and, as it flew off away from them, they noticed that it had pale tail corners; their hearts pounded as this would only be the eighth Shetland record of White's thrush. As they approached the garden the bird flew around it, this time showing its distinctive *Zoothera* underwing pattern. The bird flew up into the trees and after what seemed an eon of time dropped down into the leaf litter, shuffling and swaying from side to side as they do.

During the oil boom years of the mid-1970s to mid-1980s, Arctic gulls often graced these islands. Glaucous and Iceland gulls seemed more numerous then. On 20th November 1977 an adult Ross's gull with pinkish plumage and a neck-ring gracefully fed in Lerwick harbour to the snowy backdrop of Bressay. It was a sight to behold; it also had the company of an adult little gull. Three years later, on 13th November 1980, we were watching a first-winter ivory gull that was on the little jetty at Grutness. I showed it to my little brother Grant, who was at school in Dunrossness, and to my mum and dad. This was followed by a superb adult in Whale Firth that was feeding on an orca carcass less than a month later.

During this period John Holloway was the shop owner of Stackhoull Stores, the Fair Isle shop. He is also an ornithologist and I contacted him to see if he had any memorable reflections of that period. He told me of the time that a group of us had twitched to Fair Isle for a roller on 22nd September 1981. The bird was re-found near the shop but to see the bird meant climbing a barbed wire fence. Andrew Graham that day had a plaster cast on his leg following a recent accident. He attempted to follow everyone with his encumbrance, and eventually caught up and everyone saw the bird. John and his wife Sue were apparently helpless in stitches of laughter at the incident.

I spoke to Mark Chapman shortly before his passing and he gave me an account of the brown shrike that was also a first for Britain that he found at Grutness on 30th September 1985. He had read the weather map and although he had no transport he caught the bus to Sumburgh with brown shrike firmly on his radar. He thought that he had already found the first one at Kergord on 15th October 1981 but submitted it as an isabelline. This bird was an adult and when Mark put his bins on it he couldn't have been more pleased, especially as so many other birders got to enjoy it.

During the epoch wrynecks, barred warblers, rosefinches and red-backed shrikes were special birds that we would regularly find, as were Richard's pipits, but as previously mentioned during the early years not yellow-browed warblers. We would witness some incredible bird falls all over the islands, especially involving thrushes.

During the 1990s I didn't visit Shetland as my children were young, but I was back on the ferry north on 11th October 2002. As we were sailing out of Aberdeen Harbour I looked at my pager and it stated that a red-flanked bluetail was at Helendale, just the seventh record for Shetland. During the oil boom days this bird was the holy grail and top of our most wanted list of birds. By 8am the following morning I was standing next to my old pal Dennis Coutts watching the bird perch on a gardener's fork in a robin-like fashion. These days we see them annually and sometimes multiple times during an autumn in the archipelago.

Editorial comment: *It is notable that several of the so-called 'oil boom birders' mentioned by Ray O'Reilly went on to become distinguished and influential ornithologists who in different ways have devoted a large part of their lives to birds.*

***Clive Byers** has become an accomplished artist whose work has been published in, for example,* Birds of the Western Palearctic *and* Buntings and Sparrows. ***Mark Chapman** (1959-2018; obituary* Scot. Birds 38: 144-145*) made his home in Shetland. As well as discovering the 'first' brown shrike, Mark had an expert knowledge of Shetland's breeding birds including whimbrel, red-throated diver, and merlin.* ***Rodney Martins** (1957-2019; obituary* Brit. Birds 113: 177-178*) helped to establish the African Bird Club, Neotropical Bird Club, and Oriental Bird Club, and contributed significantly to the work of the Ornithological Society of the Middle East. As well as discovering the first Ruppell's warbler, he had a particular expertise in the birds of Yemen.* ***Craig Robson** is an acclaimed author and artist, perhaps best known for* A Field Guide to the Birds of South-East Asia *and* A Field Guide to the Birds of Thailand. ***Barry Walker**, MBE, has made his home in Peru where he established the renowned Manu Expeditions company, and is author of* Field Guide: the Birds of Machu Picchu and the Cusco Region *as well as* Peruvian Wildlife: A Visitor's Guide to the High Andes.

Discovering the Westside

Rory Tallack

I cut my birding teeth in Fair Isle and spent the following five years in Unst, so the prospect of a move to Bixter in 2011 was, at least to the birder in me, a daunting one. No one regularly birded the West Mainland. Sure, there had been a handful of good birds in the past – little bittern and roller being the pick of the bunch – but the complete list would have constituted just part of a half-decent autumn in either of the last two places I'd called home.

I've always considered myself a patch birder. I've enjoyed birding with other people on their patches, but for me nothing comes close to the experience of finding a good bird on home turf. Now I was in need of a new patch, and I began to explore the potential candidates close to home. Tresta, just a couple of miles east of my house, was the obvious choice; with its numerous plantations and established gardens it had huge potential. It was also under-watched, for the most part unwatched. I birded it fairly regularly in the early days, and I found a few decent birds – a flock of four two-barred crossbills in July 2013 being the best – but I knew it wasn't the patch for me. I like to leave a site with the impression, rightly or wrongly, that I've seen at least the majority of the birds that are present. In Tresta, and even within individual gardens in Tresta, I couldn't help feeling I'd barely scratched the surface.

After many exploratory trips to every corner of the West Mainland, I began to focus my efforts on what I call 'the westside': the area west of the Bridge of Walls, rather than the traditional definition, synonymous with 'West Mainland', which includes Tresta and everything to its west. The quality and variety of habitats there, and perhaps its paucity of large trees, appealed much more to me than either Tresta or the already well-watched Kergord. I was, however, going to have to work it out on my own. I felt like a birding pioneer, and that was exciting.

I soon gravitated towards three key areas in particular: the Dale of Walls, Melby and Norby. The Dale of Walls is a mouth-watering combination of working croft – with its obligatory muck heaps and clumps of nettles (and, unusually for Shetland, Japanese knotweed) – a handful of stunted conifers and sycamores, and a sizeable burn, its margins thick with reed canary grass, meadowsweet and flag iris. The burn meanders westwards, finally reaching its conclusion at a pebble beach, and providing tantalising views out to my very favourite birding location: Foula. Melby and Norby sit side by side in Sandness, on the north-western corner of the West Mainland. Together they offer an even richer variety of habitats, though spread over a much larger area, adding to the mix sandy beaches, crops, gardens, and two lochs that regularly hold good numbers of wildfowl and waders.

As wonderful as it sounds on paper, it soon became clear to me why no one regularly birded there: it was shit. Really shit, in fact. A quiet autumn day in Unst would have produced a good handful of migrants, probably even a lingering scarcity or two. In Fair Isle you might expect even more. But to go an entire day without seeing a single migrant was a new experience for me, and one that made me question my decision to move at all.

For the first couple of years I persevered, driving between these sites and just occasionally venturing outside my comfort zone to investigate other areas that looked promising and were easily accessible by car. I was compelled to visit at least once every month to carry out the Wetland Bird Surveys (WeBS) I'd inherited following my move. I even found a few birds. A flock of four pectoral sandpipers in 2011 doubled the previous highest Shetland count. And, in 2012, a lanceolated warbler, flushed from a roadside ditch by my car, was my first westside BBRC rarity and the first bird to draw a crowd. But one Lancy does not an autumn make, and I became increasingly disheartened with every visit. I had to change tactics.

It was in August 2013 that I sat down at my desk and started to draw lines on A4 printed maps. I chose areas that I knew relatively well already, as well as a few that I'd never been to, and devised a series of circular walking routes that took in the best habitats, including some that only became apparent as I pored over the aerial images. On 31st August I was ready, and I set out with the routes in my head and a spring in my step. That day I saw birds – lots of birds – and, to my delight, I found a citrine wagtail in an area I hadn't previously explored fully. Ok, it wasn't the rarest bird I'd found, even in Sandness, but it was enough to tell me that I might just have hit upon something.

It was around this time that Roger Riddington (my stepfather) started to join me for regular westside outings. We'd birded there together once or twice before, but I was always the guide, and lacking (as I did then) both enthusiasm and an intimate knowledge of the area, those days were never productive. Now, in addition to my new-found optimism, my wife and I had recently had our first child: a granddaughter for Roger and my mother. This meant, of course, that we could embark on more frequent westside excursions, while Mum (now Nanna) was delighted at the opportunity to pick up the slack at home.

And so began the next chapter of my westside story. Over the following years, I birded it as often as my marriage would permit, sometimes on my own but usually as a duo. Roger has his own patch in the Ness, but before long we both found ourselves to be very attached to the westside. Through trial and error, we improved upon my original birding routes and discovered new ones. We took the time to talk to the locals and earn their respect. We learned the names of the places we visited, and we named others after the birds we'd found. We compared and shared countless packed lunches. Most importantly, we found birds and plenty of them. And in the first few years, at least, we barely saw a single other birder.

The westside doesn't play by the rules. A good south-easterly blow that leaves the east coast of Shetland dripping with migrants does not necessarily produce a similar result 'out west'. Frequently, I arrive at one site to find it alive with migrants – surely a sign that an epic day is in store – only to be disappointed when other sites, even those close by, are quiet or devoid of migrants altogether. It is gloriously unpredictable, and after ten years I can't claim to have worked it out. It's fair to say that gut feeling and convenience are the key factors that dictate the timing of our visits and, fortunately for us, this has paid off. Since my first outings in 2011, we have clocked up a total of 47 West Mainland rarities (BBRC, Scottish and local), all but nine of which were 'westside' birds, by my own definition.

Melodious warbler *(Hippolais polyglotta)*, Melby, September 2018, © Rory Tallack.

The best, or at least the rarest, of these – a black-billed cuckoo at the Dale of Walls in 2017 – was a bird that I had both predicted and dreamt of finding in the preceding years, though I admit that I could have said the same about virtually every other American landbird. And while it still brings me immense satisfaction to this day – approaching that same patch of Japanese knotweed, or even just the thought of approaching it, conjures up something of the thrill of that moment – the excitement was diminished, to some extent at least, by the fact I was alone. Roger had declined an invitation to join me that morning, ostensibly because I was planning a morning visit (rather than a full day out) that had to include my WeBS sites; nonetheless, it is something he has rarely done since. My most memorable birding days, and indeed my most cherished finds, do not necessarily involve the rarest birds, but those that I've shared with others.

On one such day – perhaps the most memorable of all – we were joined by Paul Harvey and Pierre-André Crochet. It was 30th September 2017 and, as Roger's contemporary notes recall: "Having been characteristically pessimistic all the way out west, Harv's demeanour changed almost as soon as the car stopped at the Dale of Walls – it was immediately clear that there were plenty of migrants in the west of Shetland as well as in the Ness." By the end of a superb day, of laughs as well as birds, our list of finds included rustic bunting, two olive-backed pipits, and a supporting cast of bluethroat, great grey shrike, red-breasted flycatcher, three grasshopper warblers, stock dove and an impressive quantity and variety of common migrants.

I appreciate that this may be interpreted as an invitation to share in the experience of birding Shetland's westside, but that is most definitely not my intention. The American fishing writer John Gierach wrote that there are only two types of angler: the guys you're with and the assholes. For me the sentiment applies equally well to birding. Those who

Black-billed cuckoo *(Coccyzus erythrophthalmus)*, Dale of Walls, September 2017, © Rory Tallack.

know me well know that I am possessive about my patch, perhaps unhealthily so, and the inevitable increase in birders on Shetland's westside in the last few years has, for me, taken away something of the magic that made it so special.

If there *is* a moral to be gleaned from this story, it is simply this: that the 'discovery' of a new place or patch – the process of exploration by which one comes to know that place intimately – can be hugely rewarding, not just in terms of finding birds but also on a much more personal level. It is a slow process and, arguably, as all places change and evolve with time, one that never ends. Four years after leaving Bixter for the bright lights of Lerwick, I haven't been able to let the westside go. It is still my patch, and I continue to bird there more regularly than anywhere else in Shetland.

A Foula childhood in the 1950s

Sheila Gear

During our summer holidays in Foula, as a child in the 1950s, my favourite expedition was helping my father record the proportion of bridled guillemots in the island's population. First fine day, we set off. As we walked north along the road, we were continually harassed by Arctic skuas, swooping and sometimes hitting us.

Foula used to have one of the largest colonies of Arctic skuas in Britain, stretching from one end of the island to the other on the east side, and up the sides of some of the hills. Wherever you went on the low ground you were always aware of a constant ceiling of them. As small children, they had terrorised us, often forcing us to crawl along on our bellies, braced against the resounding slaps on our heads that were sure to come. Yet we loved them, loved them above all other birds. We spent hours watching them chasing and swooping in endless dog fights, skimming the ground dicing with death, hanging on the wind crying out their triumphant victory calls. We played Arctic skuas and bonxies, not cowboys and Indians.

There were plenty of other birds to take up my attention too. Now and then a meadow pipit or skylark would erupt out of the overgrown side of the road. Carefully parting the clumps of crowberry and heather, I would spy a neat nest with four small eggs or a bunch of tiny waving heads, beaks agape. As we passed bits of old dyke wheatears would hover up in the air, keeping an eye on us, but their nests were hidden out of sight; and the Fleck with its boggy tussocks was one of the best places to look out for the pretty snipe chicks, running out from right under my feet.

The Fleck used to be one of the strongholds of the Arctic skuas when my father was a boy and he lamented that there were only three pairs left there, strung out near the Clay Pool. But, to me back then, it seemed incongruous that a bird so fierce and full of life could ever have decreased. However, by the 1950s, bonxie territories packed the plateau, and they had a big club site and two small lochs nearby where they bathed. Pair after pair swooped at us as we passed through, a sudden scary rush of wind as they skimmed our heads, but they seldom actually hit.

From the Fleck, we zigzagged up the very steep, high side of the Sneug. Bonxies seemed

Bight of the Scrudhurdins and Nebbifield, Foula, © Sheila Gear, "Where, once upon a time, we spent many a happy hour counting guillemots."

sparser here. Their territories were the air space above their nests, not the actual ground surface. From up here we could look down on the third loch of the Fleck, where a pair of red-throated divers always nested, and see the two chicks swimming close to the protecting adult.

From the top of the ridge, we walked across to Nebbifield and sat there, perched on the very edge of a stunning view of the Kame, at 1,332ft Britain's second highest cliff. Puffins were everywhere. The air was buzzing with vast clouds of them circling round and round so it looked like you were peering down through dense clouds of midges. The edge of the cliff top was lined with crowds of them, massed together like black greenfly. Halfway down, every inch of the big grassy ledge of the Little Kame was covered with myriads of their burrows. There were some fulmars too, nesting here and there on the higher parts of the cliff, dotting it with white. They drifted round and round, coming to hover close over us as though curious.

Our observation place was above the Bight of the Scrudhurdins. The cliffs were not so high here, only about 600ft, but they were slightly overhanging. So it was a bit unnerving to watch my father lying stretched out on a projecting rock which gave him the best view of the cliff ledges opposite and below. My task was to keep count as he observed the guillemots through a large brass telescope. He left the body of the telescope up here throughout the summer and just took the lenses up and down.

I had a small tin containing exactly 100 tiny pebbles, and two empty tins, labelled plain and bridled. The guillemot ledges varied in size, some were long and narrow, just two or three birds deep and relatively easy to work along, but others were wider with a big bunch of tightly packed birds to be sorted through. As my father pronounced plain or bridled, I placed a pebble in the appropriate tin. When I finished the 100 pebbles, he paused while I counted the pebbles and wrote down the result.

Sometimes my father stopped as a bird hid its face under its wings and he waited patiently for it to be jogged awake by squabbling neighbours. Then I had time to sit back and enjoy my surroundings. A constant wave of sound, rising to excited crescendos, wafted up from the guillemots, composed of harsh, raucous cries but music to my ears. Puffins performed an endless pantomime along the grassy cliff edge, yawning, hiccupping and clicking bills. A wren sang, in its own Shetland dialect, very much at home on the high cliffs. Occasionally we would spot a gannet passing by offshore, and wonder if they would ever breed in Foula: on the Gaada Stack, my father thought, while I just hoped it would be somewhere that I could watch them.

I loved the smell up here, that indescribable mixture of sun-baked sandstone, the sweet scent of sea pinks and the tangy salt smell of the seabirds. Later, as an adult, I visited seabird colonies in other parts of the world, but none smelt like ours; that much-loved smell of summer. Some, in fact, smelt quite noxious, which shows the power of association.

Directly below me and all along the sides of Wester Hoevda were ledges of kittiwakes. I could look down right into their nests. Most had three chicks, mainly small and still downy. Once, to my shame, I dropped a stone down to see how long it took to hit the water. It hit a kittiwake and I watched the white body twirl down to the sea, willing it to come alive and fly, but it did not.

We counted several thousand guillemots, until my father's eyes became tired and we had to face the long plod up hill and down to get home. My legs ached but I was already plotting a further excursion, to the back of the Noup with my sister later on at night.

That evening, I set the time to wake up, carefully thumping my head on my pillow twelve times so as to wake up at midnight when I knew my parents would be safely asleep.

It is hard to fall asleep in the short, light summer nights. Outside a corncrake was calling, monotonously creaking, over and over. "Crex crex," it said, "crex crex," just under the bedroom window, or was it in the kaleyard, or maybe over there. We rarely saw them, just a glimpse of their small chicks peeping out along the edge of the cultivated rigs. I covered my ears to block out their irritating calls, wishing they would go away.

My thump alarm works. We quietly wriggled out of the bedroom window and lowered ourselves onto the back porch roof, then climbed down the wall to the ground. We went barefoot in the summer holidays so we were nimble footed. Freed from the house, we ran down to the valley and over the burn as fast as we could, in exhilaration mixed with fear our parents would find out.

On the Noup all was quiet. We disturbed occasional bonxies as we climbed up but they just lifted up a few feet off the ground with a quiet *kak* and settled down again. Most of the puffins were roosting on the sea inshore, close enough that we could pick out countless black dots against the silvery water. Now and then a gentle ripple would break, lighting up the mareel, the blue-green luminescence produced by plankton.

We headed for the Murnatoogs, a steep grassy slope running down the back of the Noup, flanked on the south side by the high cliff face of Ruski and on the north side by the Leerie Head, a jutting headland topped with broken rock. The leeries or Manx shearwaters, which gave the head its name, still nested there among the rocks, but the Murnatoogs seemed to us to be safer, although it ended abruptly at the bottom with a sheer drop.

Sunset behind Foula, © David Gifford

The slope was peppered with burrow entrances. Some were puffin burrows but most belonged to shearwaters. They looked alike but you could tell which were which by having a good sniff at them. Puffin burrows did not smell of much, maybe just a bit earthy with a tang of fish but the shearwater burrows had the warm, musky smell of the petrel family. We settled down next to a well-inhabited area and waited.

Half past one is when it gets darkest. Small shadows flickered overhead, circling and dancing: storm petrels coming home to their burrows, though most of them would be non-breeders checking options for the future. Sometimes, we would spot a Leach's petrel; bigger than the stormies, they danced a different dance.

Then out of the half darkness came the call we waited for, a shearwater coming in, calling to its mate. A heart-lifting, echoing call, one to haunt you all your life. Soon we were surrounded with incoming birds.

Though they fly long distances they are clumsy on land, landing with a thump then shuffling along almost on their bellies because their legs are set so far back. They seemed to us to be gentle birds, with mild soft eyes and they were easily caught, prey for feral cats or nocturnal bonxies. We loved to speak to them, crouching down at a burrow entrance, imitating their calls. If the burrow was inhabited by the opposite sex to our call, they would reply and we could have a conversation with them; but sometimes, if a bird of the same sex was within, they would come scuttling out to the entrance, we thought voicing their indignation. We imagined the birds with the high-pitched calls were females and the low ones males but, in fact, it is the opposite. In appearance they are rather nondescript, a dowdy black and white bird, but, to a child, a bird that speaks back to you is a special thing.

All too soon the short night was over. The shearwaters fell silent. The sheep were wending their way down the hill, baaing to each other. The Arctic skuas were stirring, males circling round to check on their chicks. Arctic terns were heading out to sea for food. The isle was coming awake. We ran back home as fast as we could, the dew-soaked ground cold on our bare feet. Our house was still asleep. Relieved, we climbed back in.

I curled up in my bed, wrapping my feet up in a bundle of blanket, and drifted off to sleep. Only my ear was still awake poking out at the edge of the cover. Listening ... listening ... Then I could hear it calling again on the edge of my dreams. "Crex crex," it said. "Crex crex."

Now, a lifetime later, the island's nights are silent. Corncrakes and shearwaters are long gone. The Arctic skuas have retreated to a small remnant group, hanging on to survival within the protection of the airstrip. You can count the puffins by the hundred not the thousand. Drop all the stones in Foula off Waster Hoevda and not hit a kittiwake. And the gannets? They nest on the ledges above the Bight of the Scrudhurdins where, once upon a time, we spent many a happy hour counting guillemots.

Snowy owls breeding in Fetlar in 1967

Dennis Coutts

Snowy owls are my favourites. I saw my first in Whalsay in 1964: about 400 yards away, this male bird looked like a tiny snowman, but when I photographed him at 40 feet, he was magnificent. Bobby Tulloch had made it possible. He suggested that I should squat in a peat cutting and then hid me under two upturned wheelbarrows and built peat around the gaps. I poked my camera lens out, aiming it optimistically at a peat stack 35 feet away. Bobby then took a wide detour around the owl, gently attempting to coax it my way. The 'ambush' idea paid off when the impressive white bird glided right on cue to the stack and I shot off three frames!

Three years later, in neighbouring Fetlar, Bobby found a snowy owl's nest with three eggs, their first recorded breeding in the wild in Britain. The event made front page news, and Bobby an overnight celebrity. Meanwhile the RSPB mounted a 24-hour guard in a hut overlooking the nest, with its access hidden from the owls, and George Waterston invited me to film the extraordinary events.

Hundreds of people came to Fetlar to enjoy viewing the Arctic visitors. One of my greatest highlights was being allowed to walk to the nest and become the first person to see the first chick hatched. The tiny, blind owlet lay with its chin cradled between two of six roundish white eggs. What a relief: had the 'Snowies' failed it would have been such an anti-climax after our high hopes, efforts and all the publicity. I then set up my photographic hide 80 yards away from the nest, and over the next fortnight Bobby moved it in to 10 yards. Six chicks now occupied the nest and having hatched at about day-and-a-half intervals were all of different sizes; one egg failed to hatch and sadly the smallest chick did not survive.

By the time the hide was finally in its position, I'd photographed several weddings and was eager to swap brides for birds. At 6am one fine morning I met the warden on duty at the watch hut and he accompanied me to the hide. As we walked the female flew from the nest, but the male glided in low over our heads, barking, then landed a few yards away still barking. As I entered the hide the warden headed back to the hut and had gone only 100 yards when the male flew back to his regular look-out post, a large rock. Within minutes the female returned to the nest, glanced briefly at my lens and became pre-occupied with the chicks.

Snowy owls (*Bubo scandiacus*), Fetlar, 1967, © Dennis Coutts, "Of all my birding highlights, my time with the snowy owls was indeed a privilege."

Three hours later the chicks' heads suddenly swayed from side to side excitedly. I pressed the ciné camera button: in a flash the male swept in clutching a small rabbit. He transferred it from his talons to his bill – passed the prey to his mate in a quick tug-of-war – and left. He returned to his rock and remained there all day, doing little but ducking when Arctic skuas dive-bombed only inches from his head.

I switched to a telephoto lens for close-ups of the female while she was distracted by the rabbit. She raised the feathers that normally mask the bill so they bristled like whiskers, and with her head down, began to rip up the rabbit. Pausing for a moment, she rolled her yellow eyes up to the lens with a drop-dead stare. That look combined with those whiskers reminded me of my old 'walrus-moustached' grandpa who had been a Greenland whaler back in the 1880s.

Over time five chicks eventually dispersed from the nest, still covered in grey down. This enabled them to blend in with the surrounding rocks, and hide when they heard an adult's alarm call. Apart from the bare intertarsal joints, their legs were feathered white, like woolly socks. If they got up to scurry off, I had to laugh: the pink skin of 'heels' flashed through holes in their 'socks'! During September the chicks began to fly and then resembled their mother, although the white feathers were more heavily barred with brown. The snowy owls nested in Fetlar over another eight seasons, but 1967 was their most successful.

I am forever grateful to George Waterston for entrusting me with this once-in-a-lifetime assignment. The resulting 16mm film, 'The Snowy Owls of Fetlar', featured in the RSPB's regular winter shows and was also shown on television. Its international reach was confirmed when a German birdwatcher I had met previously in Fetlar phoned me after seeing it on TV in Berlin.

Of all my birding highlights, my time with the snowy owls was indeed a privilege.

Editorial comment: *Following Bobby Tulloch's discovery of a nest in 1967, snowy owls bred in Fetlar until 1975 and a total of 23 chicks fledged. A paper summarising these events was published by Robinson & Becker (1986). Andrew Harrop's wife remembers being taken to look for the Fetlar snowy owls as a girl. On Andrew's first visit to Shetland in autumn 1980, using public transport and hitch-hiking, he arrived in Unst to look for the black-browed albatross (which he missed). As he walked up the road from Belmont towards the Uyeasound junction he unexpectedly saw a female snowy owl and still remembers being surprised by its size and piercing yellow eyes. Every encounter with this species is special.*

Since the 1990s records in Shetland have become more irregular, though there has been an encouraging recent increase involving four to six individuals during 2018-2020. Snowy owl is a sporadic breeder in the West Palearctic, and may not breed anywhere in Europe during poor years, so the probability of another breeding attempt in Shetland seems low.

An email from Switzerland

23rd July 2013
Malcie Smith

I guess I'm a little off-brief here, as my most memorable birding day did not involve the arrival of an ultra-rare vagrant bird, but a rather short email from Switzerland ...

When I first started working as the Fetlar warden for RSPB in May 1998, one of my key roles was to monitor breeding red-necked phalaropes and to try to provide the best possible habitat we could within the nature reserve. I soon found myself intrigued by these tiny birds which were both waders and seabirds – two of my favourite bird groups. They were just so weird. They did not establish breeding territories, the males did all the incubating and chick-rearing and at the end of their very contracted breeding season, they moulted from their quite gaudy summer plumage into the typically marine uniform of white with a bit of black. Suitably dressed, they spent the rest of the year bobbing about in tropical or sub-tropical seas in, often, massive foraging flocks.

Although red-necked phalaropes breed throughout the sub-Arctic, most of them winter in just three key areas: the Arabian Sea, the Pacific coast of South America and the waters around the East Indies. It was assumed that the relatively small population of Shetland-breeders joined their Scandinavian cousins in the closest of these sites – the Arabian Sea. Ringing recoveries had clearly shown that this population did indeed spend their winters there.

RSPB initiated a ringing and colour-ringing project in the early 1990s and I continued this work which Mark O'Brien (RSPB researcher) and my predecessor Dave Suddaby had started. One of the aims of this project was to try to confirm the wintering quarters of Shetland's phalaropes. Despite the ringing of hundreds of birds (mostly as chicks) over the years, only a tiny number were ever seen outside Shetland. Two juvenile birds which I had ringed in Fetlar were reported as autumn migrants in the south of England and the south of France respectively. This didn't tell us much – only confirming that they migrate south in autumn. This wasn't enormously helpful, but perhaps hinted that they were indeed heading to the Arabian Sea as suspected? A third Shetland-ringed bird, an adult, was recorded in Lewis in May 2018.

It was clear that we needed some modern technology. I contacted scientists at British Antarctic Survey for advice. In the early 1990s an engineer called Vsevolod Afanasyev and researchers from BAS had developed geolocators small enough to attach to birds. Geolocators record daylength, so provided the tag knew what time it was, they could calculate latitude and longitude. The birds involved however were wandering albatrosses and were big enough to carry the 30g gadgets on their backs. This is just a few grams lighter than the weight of a phalarope. I asked when they thought they'd be small enough to attach to phalaropes, i.e. 1.0g or less. They were polite enough not to laugh at me, but suggested that it may be "many years" before battery technology allowed such small devices to be developed. I waited patiently and immediately got my hands on ten 0.6g geolocators as soon as they became available in 2012.

The tags were provided by Vogelwarte (Swiss Ornithological Institute). Apart from being incredibly lightweight, they were also quite cheap to produce. The downside is that the data they gather cannot be transmitted by satellite, meaning the tags have to be retrieved from the host birds. We recognised from an early stage that retrieving tags was going to be much more challenging than putting them on.

Ron Summers, an RSPB researcher with a special interest in high latitude waders who had experience of fitting tracking devices onto purple sandpipers, trained me in attaching tags using a harness. The harness sat on the back of the bird and was held in place with loops which went around the birds' legs. For training purposes we used a dunlin from Ron's freezer!

Suitably trained and armed with a small box of geolocators, we captured ten phalaropes (six males and four females) on the RSPB nature reserve in Fetlar in June 2012. They were caught by a combination of mist-netting and nest-traps. Attaching the geolocators was a bit of a fiddle to say the least, and we also fitted metal BTO rings and plastic colour-rings to birds which were not already ringed. We kept a close eye on these birds over the following few weeks and it was apparent that the tags were not affecting the behaviour of their hosts as they continued to forage and breed as expected. The only real concern we had was that a couple of birds had managed to lose their tags. One male was seen minus his tag five days after it had been fitted. Remarkably, Martha Devine spotted the tiny, almost transparent, tag lying by the side of a remote pool several miles away from the bird's nesting site while she was surveying breeding red-throated divers. The tag was still working, so we refitted it onto another male in July.

The following summer, after a rather anxious winter, many hours were spent trying to relocate and capture birds tagged in 2012. Two birds, a male and a female, had lost their geolocators during the winter. A female, who clearly still had her tag attached, could not be recaptured despite many efforts. During one recapture attempt, after relocating her, we gently herded her towards the mist nets – this is easier said than done – and she flew into a net, but bounced off and disappeared back into the dense vegetation! We never did manage to trap her.

Eventually, on 19th June, myself and Martha, after several hours spent at a key phalarope site trying to relocate tagged birds, caught a glimpse of a colour-ringed male which appeared to be a combination we were looking for (red on the left leg and yellow on the right). We eventually managed to get a closer look at him – not only was he one of the birds we were looking for, but we were pretty sure we could see the tag on his back. What's more, his behaviour indicated that he was incubating. This was really exciting; incubating males are much easier to catch as you can use a nest-trap which nearly always works, unlike mist nets which are very hit-and-miss. We sat back to watch from a distance

Red-necked phalarope *(Phalaropus lobatus)*, Fetlar, June 2013, © George Petrie.

and within 15 minutes, with fingers tightly crossed, we watched him sneak onto his nest which was just a few metres away from where we'd seen him. Bingo! I carefully weighed and measured his eggs to confirm that he'd been incubating for at least a few days – this is important because if he'd just started incubating, there was a risk of him abandoning the nest if disturbed.

The following day Dave Okill and George Petrie from the Shetland Ringing Group made another trek to Fetlar to help with retrapping 'Red-Yellow'. We placed the trap over the nest, carefully stored his clutch of four eggs in an insulated box and replaced the clutch with Dave's home-made clay dummy eggs. This was essential, as we didn't want to risk damaging his eggs while retrapping him. We only had to wait about ten minutes for him to squeeze through the gap in the net and let him settle down onto his clutch of 'eggs'. I then bombed it from our watching location to the nest trap, desperately trying not to trip up on the wet uneven ground and easily got hold of him and placed him in a bird bag, which I tied really, really carefully before taking him to the delighted team. After many whoops of relief and a wee bit of delighted swearing, we cut the loops of the harness and argued over who had the most secure zipped pocket to carry the tag home.

The tag was posted off to Herbert Stark at Vogelwarte and we had to wait for an excruciating four weeks to get a reply. On 23rd July, after a morning's fieldwork, I came back to The Baelans – RSPBs house/office in Fetlar – to catch up on some paperwork. In my

Red-necked phalarope, South Mainland, May 2021, © Rebecca Nason.

inbox was an email from Herbert. There had been lots of communications with Vogelwarte, so I wasn't especially excited until I read that Herbert's colleague, Erich Bächler, had done a 'quick and dirty' analysis of the data extracted from the tag and: "The migration route is quite interesting (especially for us!). The bird migrated via Iceland to Canada and along the US coast to South America (west coast). Did you know that from ringing?"

After nearly falling off my chair, I reread the email a couple of times before getting in touch with everyone who'd been involved in the project to tell them the news. The results were published in *Ibis*, the journal of the British Ornithologists' Union and attracted quite a lot of media attention. It also inspired a song-cycle performed by 2,000 school children and several young Peruvian musicians in the Royal Albert Hall, London, in 2016, and later in Carlisle and Lerwick.

Further tags were fitted on phalaropes in 2014 and 2015 to try to get more migration tracks to firm up what Red-Yellow had previously told us. These were desperately frustrating years, beset with the now-familiar problems of tags being lost from birds and failed attempts to recapture those birds which had returned with tags intact. We had one last attempt where we tried a different attachment method in 2016. Two of these birds, 'Green-Orange' and 'Brown-Blue', both males, were recaptured in June 2017. The latter of these birds was caught by Phil Harris in a spectacular horizontal dive using a hand-net. The data from these birds both showed remarkably similar migration routes to Red-Yellow's 2012-13 journey.

Subsequent projects run by other researchers which used geolocators attached to breeding red-necked phalaropes confirmed that birds breeding in Iceland and Greenland followed a similar route to Shetland birds, while those tagged in Norway, Sweden, Finland and Russia wintered in the Arabian Sea. Many ornithologists in Iceland had previously guessed that their phalaropes migrated west, but it had never been proven before.

Many people were involved in this project. Key members of the team were Dave Okill, George Petrie, Roger Riddington, Phil Harris and Pete Ellis from the Shetland Ringing Group. The project would not have succeeded without the technical skills of storm petrel expert Mark Bolton and support from Jerry Wilson and Ron Summers from RSPB.

Incidentally, several years before this project started, Jerry Wilson and some of his research colleagues ran a model which looked at fluctuations in return rates of our population and compared this with environmental conditions in the Pacific off Peru and the Arabian Sea and found a strong correlation with the Pacific. Jerry was, therefore, pretty much the only person who successfully predicted the wintering quarters of Shetland's breeding phalaropes.

Storm petrels night and day

Will Miles

Part 1: Two Swinhoe's petrels in Fair Isle

Night-time storm petrel ringing sessions have been carried out annually by the wardens in Fair Isle since 1957, and over the years more than 40,000 storm petrels have been ringed. Typically, playback of storm petrel and Leach's petrel calls has been used to attract the birds in. Swinhoe's petrel calls were first played in 2011, when I included a sound track or two of Swinhoe's chatter-calls on a playlist with tracks of the usual two species. The Swinhoe's calls had been given to me by Magnus Robb in 2007 on St Kilda, and later featured in the book *Petrels night and day* produced by Magnus and The Sound Approach Team. Playing Swinhoe's calls during storm petrel ringing sessions was always entirely speculative, a naïve roll of the dice, based on simple curiosity and the extremely unlikely odds that maybe one day a wandering individual might be passing at night. And in retrospect, it all still seems so impossibly unlikely ...

On the night of 21st/22nd July 2013 conditions for a 'stormie' ringing session in Fair Isle were absolutely perfect. Thick fog covered the island, creating exceptionally dark conditions; the wind was very light, with just a breath of an easterly; and the sea was flat calm, so the night was also very quiet – ideal for play-back calls and real calls to be clearly audible. Just after midnight, the bird observatory team set up two mist nets by North and South Haven, just down the hill from the observatory, each net with a speaker system underneath it playing mp3 tracks of a range of petrel calls. The South Haven speaker had the following track sequence playing on repeat: Leach's – Leach's – storm – storm – Swinhoe's – Leach's – storm – Leach's – Swinhoe's – Madeiran – storm. The Swinhoe's track comprised both male and female chatter-calls, but also had streaked shearwater calls quietly in the background. That night, Richard Cope and Teresa Donohue supervised the North Haven net, David Parnaby and Noa Eden were on the South Haven net, and Billy Dykes was ferrying petrels from the nets to the ringing garages, where I was based, ringing and releasing birds. Soon after the speakers went on (at about 12.15am) storm petrels began to fly in, and by the end of the night a total of 44 had been trapped and ringed, plus two Leach's.

At 2.30am, near to the end of the session, I happened to walk out of the garages and heard Swinhoe's calls coming from the speaker under the South Haven net, but Swinhoe's calls also coming from an area south of the net, just offshore. For a brief moment, I thought the calls from offshore must somehow be another recording or an echo, but I soon realised they were not in synchrony with the track being played, were totally pure (no streaked shearwaters in the background), were not coming from the speaker under the North Haven net, and that the source was in mid-air and moving rapidly around. The penny dropped and I ran towards South Haven shouting, "There's a Swinhoe's calling!" (or language to that effect).

Everyone quickly assembled on the low cliff top, listening. The bird continued to call very loudly from somewhere close by in the Haven, but it now seemed to be stationary, presumably having landed on the water or a nearby rock. Suddenly, the sound system automatically switched track from Swinhoe's to Madeiran petrel, and with Madeiran playing the bird soon went silent. Everybody had been waiting for it to fly in to the net, but now it had stopped calling we all imagined it flying back out to sea. The soundtrack was quickly switched back to Swinhoe's calls and the result was instantaneous – the bird resumed calling. David ran to the observatory to get a sound recording device, but before he could return the bird went silent again and was heard no more. It had called on and off for about ten minutes in total, somewhere nearby in the foggy night, but at no point was it ever seen.

We waited until well after dawn had passed before packing up that morning, but the bird had gone. The whole team had heard it, no one had any doubts about the identification, and everyone was buzzing from the experience; but we also hoped that the story would not end there with just the calls, the darkness, and nothing more.

From 22nd to 26th July the weather was calm in Fair Isle and the observatory team were able to do storm petrel sessions every night. It was an excellent few days, with over 150 storm petrels and four Leach's petrels trapped and ringed, magnificent views of a pod of four orcas on the afternoon of 25th, and the discovery of a flock of eight two-barred crossbills on the 26th. The week was characterised by drifting fog, thickening on the 26th and greatly reducing light and visibility for the stormie session that night. It was the first night with similar conditions to those when the Swinhoe's petrel had been heard; however, the fog was *even* thicker and the air increasingly heavy and brooding, like that before a tropical storm. Fair Isle was conjuring a rare atmosphere. Never before had the darkness felt so charged and promising. As I sat at the net that night, waiting for the first petrels to come in, it was as though the island was saying "get ready".

The nightshift team on the 26th/27th was Kieran Lawrence, Tegan Newman, Daniel McGibbon, Teresa, Noa and me. Two nets were put up, in an 'L' shape facing east into South Haven and, as on 22nd, the speaker system under the nets was programmed to repeat various storm petrel calls, including Swinhoe's. The night ticked along nicely and by 1.25am we had caught 32 storm petrels and a Leach's petrel.

At that time, I happened to be at the net with Daniel when suddenly we heard the calls of a Swinhoe's petrel seemingly very near to us, just a few feet away. We were at the middle of the net, having just extracted a storm petrel, but we swiftly moved aside in case the Swinhoe's came in. Almost immediately, we saw a large storm petrel fly into the mesh just above the speaker. I quickly reached the bird and gently took hold of it. It felt far larger than a storm petrel but slightly smaller than any Leach's I had ever held. It was in the middle shelf

Swinhoe's petrel *(Hydrobates monorhis)*, Fair Isle, August 2013, © Will Miles, "Arguably, Swinhoe's is the most enigmatic seabird of the Atlantic."

of the net, just sitting in the pocket, and cautiously I parted its wing tips to look at the rump ... no white. The bird was all-dark, like a shadow in the mesh, and my brain began to spin. Fighting to keep a grip on reality, I carefully extracted the bird from the net and placed it in a bird-bag, I turned off the speaker system, asked everyone to meticulously double-check that there were no other petrels in the net (there were none), and we closed the mist-nets.

The storm petrel was ringed and released before I then sat down to examine the dark-rumped bird in the light. It had to be a Swinhoe's, but I wanted to check all the features to be certain. They were all there. Unlike a dream, it really was one! We took the bird and the ringing equipment up the hill to the observatory for detailed measurements to be taken. It was ringed and measured carefully, as an appreciative crowd gathered, formed of observatory staff and guests, plus many islanders (some in nightwear) who had driven up the isle to see it – an amazingly unusual seabird and the first rarity in Fair Isle to appear in total darkness.

The bird was soon taken back to South Haven to be released. With it sitting quietly on the open palm of my hand, I stood facing the sea, letting it reacclimatise to the natural environment, free to go when it was perfectly ready. And after a couple of minutes, it shuffled onto my fingertips, opened its wings, and flew off strongly into the night. As this happened however, Deryk Shaw, Rob Hughes and I heard a distinctive chatter-call come from far offshore. We only heard it once, very faintly, somewhere out in the gloom, but it had sounded like another Swinhoe's petrel.

During the following days, the weather in Fair Isle remained calm and settled and storm petrel ringing sessions were carried out in the early hours of 28th, 30th and 31st July and 1st, 5th and 6th August. During these sessions 374 storm petrels and seven Leach's petrels were trapped and ringed, but there was no further sign of the Swinhoe's. On the night of 6th/7th August, the weather was slightly overcast but again very calm, and the observatory team set out for another petrel session at 11.30pm. The usual mist-net was set up facing into South Haven, a sound system was placed under the net, and soon a steady stream of storm petrels were being trapped and ringed (86 in total that night) and at least two Leach's petrels were heard calling frequently overhead (2013 was a record season for Leach's petrels in Fair Isle, with a final total of 20 ringed).

At 2.20am, Kieran was sitting at the south end of the net and I was at the north end, when a large storm petrel hit the mesh close to where I was standing. Given that Leach's petrels had been heard calling virtually all night, indeed within the previous two minutes, and there had been a total lack of any Swinhoe's calls, I approached the bird expecting it to be a Leach's. The first things I saw were its legs, neither of which was ringed. In the hand, it felt about the right size for a Leach's, but on turning the bird over I saw that everything about it was dark. It was *another* dark-rumped storm petrel!

In total disbelief, I extracted the bird and placed it in a bird-bag, Kieran turned off the sound system, we checked that there were no more petrels in the net, and then furled the net shut. We took the bird over to the ringing garages and quickly finished processing and releasing the last batch of storm petrels. Then, for the second time in eleven days, I sat down to check the features of a dark-rumped storm petrel and confirmed the mind-bending truth: that it really was a *second* Swinhoe's petrel. At that moment, I looked up at the faces around the room and every single one was beaming happiness.

As with the first Swinhoe's, the second bird was quickly ringed, measured in detail and photographed, then taken back to South Haven to be released. Standing at the edge of the Haven, I carefully placed the petrel onto the open hands of Dennis Coutts. It sat quietly for a few minutes on Dennis's binocular-worn palms, then fluffed itself up slightly, spread its wings, and darted away to the open sea.

The Fair Isle Swinhoe's petrels extended the intriguing series of records of the species occurring in the Atlantic Ocean that date back to 1983 and include the famous 'Tyne petrels'. To date, the only known breeding sites of Swinhoe's petrels are in the Pacific Ocean, around the Sea of Japan and the Yellow Sea, and the only known wintering area is the northern Indian Ocean. Encounters with Swinhoe's in the Atlantic never fail to amaze and never fail to raise questions. Is there an Atlantic breeding population? Does the species 'wander' into the Atlantic around the tip of South Africa, or perhaps even via the Red Sea and then overland into the Mediterranean? Why do individuals return again and again to the same ringing site and sound-lure, when storm petrels and Leach's petrels do not? Did more than two individuals visit Fair Isle calling in 2013?

Arguably, Swinhoe's is the most enigmatic seabird of the Atlantic. For birdwatchers and ornithologists, the species has an alluring aura of rarity and mystique, and gaining answers to the many questions raised by the Atlantic records presents a considerable challenge. DNA and call sonogram analyses revealed that both of the Fair Isle birds were male, and the genetic analyses confirmed they were not siblings. The first bird was not seen again in 2013, or in 2014 or 2015, but was re-trapped in Fair Isle in both 2016 and 2017. The second bird returned frequently to Fair Isle in 2013 and 2014 but was not seen thereafter. Tracking storm petrels at sea using ultra-lightweight miniature data loggers and GPS trackers is now possible. In future, these developing techniques combined with the species' site fidelity and responsiveness to sound-lures, could perhaps be used to help us understand the occurrence of this tiny seabird on the opposite side of the world to its known Pacific breeding sites.

Part 2:
Two Wilson's petrels off northwest Shetland

The events that follow were the result of different people with different skills all working together and were an entirely collective endeavour and experience. Therefore, this piece is written in the third person.

Wilson's petrel is considered extremely rare in Scotland: to date, there have been fewer than ten accepted records. It is the only bird on the Scottish list with an Antarctic breeding distribution and, if all this were not inspiration enough to look for one, also, hardly ever has the species been photographed in Scottish waters.

There is a photograph of one in *The Birds of Scotland* and *The Birds of Shetland* that is quietly awesome. It is Paul Sclater's at-sea photo, taken from a horribly rolling boat, before the age of digital photography. It depicts the third record for Scotland and first for Shetland, delicately hang-gliding low over the water, yellow-webbed feet dangling – seen in August 1993, 46km northwest of the Ramna Stacks. For those who search for strange seabirds in Scottish waters, this photo has long been inspirational.

Offshore seabird pelagics from Shetland require a substantial amount of luck to ever happen, since many unlikely factors have to perfectly align, not least calm seas and gentle weather conditions across sea area Fair Isle. For several years, Phil Harris, Glen Tyler and Will Miles had discussed the possibility of doing an offshore pelagic to the northwest of Shetland in Phil's boat, *Ayda Ruby II*. One of the golden rules of seabird pelagics is to go in a fast boat with very comfy, forward-facing seats, and *Ayda Ruby II* is perfect for the job. With a fast, comfy boat you get to your chosen destination relatively quickly, the journey is less arduous, the likelihood of vomit is (potentially) reduced, and the chances of you feeling fresh and alive and fully able to concentrate when you get out there are much improved. So, we had the right boat. But what about everything else?

During the second week of August 2020, high-pressure created calm conditions across much of sea area Fair Isle, after strong westerlies earlier in the month. The forecasts showed that the sea state and weather could be ideal for a pelagic on August 10th, so a plan was rapidly hatched. Phil identified a promising-looking offshore location to the northwest of Shetland, where the seabed shelved relatively very steeply from 400m to 500m depth, potentially creating an upwelling hotspot. He also sourced the ingredients and equipment for chumming, namely two massive boxes of herring, a large bottle of salmon oil, a loose-weave hessian sack, and a laundry basket to hang it all in over the side. On the evening of 9th August he checked and fuelled-up the boat, then left the herring to defrost and 'ripen' overnight at Will's house rather than at his own! Meanwhile, Glen spent the evening cooking up popcorn (it floats on the sea's surface and when soaked in fish oil gives pelagic petrels something juicy to pick at). It seemed we were all set, but would the weather hold good?

Very luckily, it did. There was just a light easterly wind and gentle roll on the sea as we headed off northwest on 10th August, out into the Atlantic from Fethaland, the most northerly tip of mainland Shetland. Also on board were seabird gurus Mick Mellor, Paul Harvey and Jenny Sturgeon. On the way out, Glen prepared the chum, mashing the herring into fish soup using the 'chum hammer' (an immense plastic mallet he'd brought especially) and adding salmon oil and popcorn to finish. About one kilometre out, a sooty shearwater suddenly flew by at close range (we took it as a good omen); then, further offshore we passed many puffins and fulmars, but only a few storm petrels. We reached the spot that Phil had selected, 66km out, switched off the engines, put the chum basket over the side and began to slowly drift westwards with the wind, out over deeper and deeper water.

The chum did its job. It produced a slick of fish oil behind us to the east and a strong fishy aroma in the air that was blown westwards ahead of us. Seabirds began to appear over the horizon to the west, flying straight at us. Mostly fulmars at first, many gathering alongside the boat, but also more and more storm petrels. These tended to fly past the boat at close range but then slow down over the slick behind us, flitting back and forth, dipping down and occasionally foot-pattering as they foraged along the slick, gradually moving away eastwards into the wind. It was amazing to watch them appear ahead of the boat and home-in on the chum behind it – at times there were storm petrels all around us!

At 1.25pm several of us picked up a small storm petrel coming in from the west that seemed to have an unusually large white rump and plain blackish underwings. It switched direction and flew ahead of the boat, keeping well away from us, never closer than 80m. As it became more visible, forward on the port side, there was an explosion of expletives from Will, then: "Wilson's!" It had short, pale grey greater-covert bars, a square-cut black tail, a small, delicate head and bill structure, and its band-shaped white rump curved far under the body. Unexpectedly, it quickly turned and flew off southwest, completely avoiding the boat and the chum. As it did so, Will got a few long-range photos. Its flight action was very distinctive, with more hanging and gliding than the storm petrels – though it was still very quick – and its wing shape was broader and less angled, often with the trailing edge of both wings held completely straight. Unusually for Wilson's, at no point did it show a toe-

Wilson's petrel *(Oceanites oceanicus)*, August 2020, © Will Miles.

projection beyond the tail, including in any of the photos. Our position was 61° 7.693'N, 2° 5.522' W. The whole sequence lasted no more than 30 seconds, with the bird often out of sight, hidden between waves.

Some of us began to celebrate, but it soon became clear that Mick had not got on the bird. He took it well, but we all knew it was a very special seabird and that missing it had to hurt, also that the chances of seeing another were exceedingly slim. We motored back to the top of the slick, renewed the chum, and repeated the drift. But apart from a couple of sooty shearwaters, things seemed to have really quietened down. For long periods now there were no storm petrels. At 2.45pm the decision was made to give it another half-hour but then head home.

At 2.53pm a small flurry of storm petrels came in from the west, shortly followed by a bird that set Phil and Will bellowing, "Wilson's! – Mick! – Wilson's!" But Mick was already on it. The bird flew rapidly towards the boat, came close in around the stern, then began foraging over the slick less than 10m away. All the features of Wilson's petrel could be clearly seen, including a very distinctive toe-projection visible at all times. It was the perfect Wilson's. It glided, flicked, foot-pattered and pirouetted across the water, swept back around the stern, then back to the chum again, always at close range. It stayed near the boat for several minutes, allowing many photographs to be taken, then headed off eastwards slowly up the slick. Our position was 61° 9.431' N, 2° 5.593' W.

The unlikeliness of the sighting seemed incredible and everyone was smiling. Sightings of Wilson's petrel like that surely only ever happened off Scilly, but we were off Shetland! Happily, we decided to call it a day. As we headed off east though, we saw the bird one last time, still foraging over the slick: tiny, quick and Antarctic.

Back in Lerwick that evening, Phil, Jenny and Will were tidying up the boat when a sports car drew up at the harbour. The owner stepped out, walked over, got the story and warmly congratulated us. It was Paul Sclater: a nice touch to end a good day.

Postscript: Phil, Glen and Will organised a further two pelagics in *Ayda Ruby II* in August 2021, to the same offshore area, again using chum to attract seabirds, and again with the aim of finding Wilson's petrel. The first trip, on 3rd August, resulted in close-range sightings of an adult pomarine skua with full 'tail spoons', four Arctic skuas, three Manx shearwaters, five sooty shearwaters, over 200 storm petrels, and the highlight of the trip, a Leach's petrel foraging 'nighthawk-style' over the chum slick within a few metres of the boat. The second trip, on 10th August, was the most successful pelagic to date in Shetland waters. Sightings included three Arctic skuas, seven sooty shearwaters, one 'blue' fulmar, 180 storm petrels, four Atlantic white-sided dolphins, one minke whale and one porbeagle shark. However, the star species of the trip were an adult Sabine's gull that fed on Will's leftover sandwiches, and, late in the afternoon at very close range, another Wilson's petrel! Three Wilson's petrels in two years from just three bespoke pelagics to look for the species suggests that small numbers regularly summer in Shetland's offshore waters, and that this Antarctic breeder is more common in the far north in summer than previously thought.

Living the dream – Shetland style

Rebecca Nason

My assistant warden/seabird officer days in Fair Isle seem a lifetime away now: the hazy memories of daily census, the feelings of youthful optimism, of fitness, of being on top of the birding world; or at least enthusiastically at the top of Britain anyway, on the magic isle – anything was possible!

However, although much changes over time, nearly 20 years on several things still remain permanent fixtures, which I find rather comforting. Being a passionate birder, totally in love with the birding scene and lifestyle of the northern isles, as well as the photographic opportunities experienced in my two years working at FIBO, I guess my direction was pretty much cast. I bought a house in Lerwick with Phil Harris, who I met in Fair Isle in 2003, and we moved to Shetland from Suffolk in late 2013, virtually nine years to the day after the deliriously happy chestnut-eared bunting and rufous-tailed robin autumn of 2004. After experiencing birding in Fair Isle over those years, nowhere other than Fair Isle or another Shetland island could match and satisfy the need for the quality and intensity of northern isles birding. Like many wardens and assistants before me, nothing beats UK birding here; moving to Shetland was a must. Moving to the main town of Lerwick, in Mainland Shetland, was due to finding the right garden (and house) at the right time.

Bird photography has progressively dominated my time and enjoyment out in the field over the years. Memories are now often focused on what I was photographing well or not photographing well at the time. Those 'early days' working in Fair Isle now seem to be encapsulated forever for me with one particular image I took, that of the rufous-tailed robin, a first for the Western Palearctic, that turned up on 23rd October 2004 and was only seen by a handful of birders. The extreme rarity value, which continues to this day, coupled with the extreme luck of turning around the corner of a drystone wall only to come face to face with the otherwise elusive, skulking bird right out in the open in front of me is surely my top birding and photography highlight from Fair Isle to date. I think we had only just worked out what the bird we were getting brief views of was when I took that picture, having previously thought a *Catharus* thrush was most likely. It doesn't get much better than to see and photograph a bird of that magnitude on the magic isle.

Rufous-tailed robin *(Larvivora sibilans)*, Fair Isle, October 2004, © Rebecca Nason.

For the majority of those pre-Shetland years, any savings were put towards Fair Isle trips, generally twice a year in spring and autumn as well as a couple of times in summer to help with seabird work. Although we missed many a rarity living off isle, we still seemed to have luck on our side. I managed to claw back my first Siberian rubythroat in 2005 after missing one in 2003 due to finishing my Fair Isle contract early and heading down to Scilly, though Savannah sparrow still remains an enigma. Other Fair Isle highlights that really stand out include seeing and photographing the citril finch, another first for Britain, in June 2008, first at The Haa then at Barkland along a wire fence. Another came with finding my own White's thrush the same autumn. Nothing stokes the 'mega fire' like a far-eastern *Zoothera*, and looking over a wall into Quoy garden with camera raised that October, whilst trying to keep up with a sprightly bluethroat, my dream find appeared like a giant, crazy patterned mistle thrush, pink legs bold against the brown peaty soil, ear cocked listening for worms. That heart-stopping, mega-find moment is a particularly good one and one I'm sure any bird finder is constantly keen to replicate. Those birding 'holidays' to Fair Isle were extremely special, we were living our 'best life', or at least our 30s anyway.

Time spent in mainland Shetland was minimal over those years, though a massive birding highlight we often think back to is when we re-found the pine grosbeak at Collafirth with Tim Cleeves on 2nd February 2013, the same year we moved to Shetland permanently. We were due on the NorthLink that night at the end of our holiday, as we headed up to scour suitable habitat with Tim who had pulled out of joining Ann on his flight south the day before, to do the same. I remember Tim on the phone whilst searching trees from

Rufous-tailed robin in a typical Fair Isle setting, October 2004, © Rebecca Nason.

the roadside at Saltoo, and Phil and I working, enthusiastically, a garden that seemed very suitable. On finding little, I felt downcast and as we started to make our way back up through the garden I took out my phone and found pine grosbeak, not having thought about its call or song until that moment. I played it: it was beautiful, quite redwing-like and fluty. To my astonishment, from deep within a pine belt nearby, the same faint, almost subsong version came drifting back in the winds over the garden towards us. This is what dreams are made of! We rushed over to the pines and before long the tangerine-orange and grey form of a chunky first-winter grosbeak appeared on the edges of the top branches above us. Soon the three of us were watching this stunning bird as it drank from a puddle just feet away.

The autumn saw us move to Shetland, swiftly followed by the first big autumn surprise with Mike Pennington's discovery of a first-winter Cape May warbler on Unst, seen from 23rd October to 2nd November. Spending quality time as a new 'local' with a bird of that magnitude, watching 'twitchers' charter planes and depart as quickly as they had arrived, gave me an enormous sense of commitment to our move and confirmation that we had done the right thing. It was a privilege to spend quality time with massive UK rarities, and the feeling was like that I had experienced on Fair Isle over a decade before. We were not hedging our birding luck on a few weeks of the year, or spending hundreds, thousands even, on chartering planes for rarities. They were on our doorstep.

Near the end of the year, I was carrying out greylag goose counts on the outskirts of Lerwick in November when I raised my bins to a number of redwing perched up on a low barbed wire fence. I was shocked to see a first-winter female black-throated thrush among

Siberian rubythroat *(Calliope calliope)*, Levenwick, October 2014, © Rebecca Nason, "Dream encounters like this are what Shetland is all about for me."

them! In Shetland anything can happen and when you least expect it; on this occasion a damp, cold November day in suburban Lerwick.

Perhaps my best rarity shot to date was captured the next autumn, hailed as the best rarity photograph of the year by Rare Bird Alert, which went viral online the evening I showcased the shot. The image was of a stunning male Siberian rubythroat, front-on, right out in the open, taken at Levenwick on 8th October 2014, the last day the bird was seen after being found originally on 4th October by Dan Pointon. A special bird and day indeed, watching it hopping through low garden vegetation; views were brief, it gave the skulking mannerisms and appearance of what I imagine these birds are like on the forest floors of eastern Siberia, the brief shocking red amongst the browns of the leaf litter only heightened its intense appeal. However, on this particular morning fleeting views were peppered with incredible views, as the upright, buoyant chat made irregular dashes out onto a driveway to feed, stopping momentarily before darting back into cover again. I got lucky with that shot and it is by far my most memorable rarity image taken since moving to the isles. Dream encounters like this are what Shetland is all about for me.

That first full autumn in Shetland produced a fine suite of birds, from pied wheatear, to myrtle warbler, eastern Bonelli's warbler to lanceolated warbler. We also saw three red-flanked bluetails, with Phil and I finding one each. Our earlier June trip to Fair Isle that year had been our best for a while too, as while watching a smart bridled tern in South Harbour Phil called out a laughing gull, which was quite literally on the same rocks. It was we who were laughing that night at the bar and log call.

Hermit thrush *(Catharus guttatus)*, Noss, April 2017, © Rebecca Nason.

In 2015 we welcomed our wonderful little Ayda 'Ruby' to the world, which obviously changed our daily lives dramatically, as well as buying a boat and starting the now famous Noss Boat – Shetland Seabird Tours. It was a little harder to get to the rarities and photographic opportunities in those early baby years, though one particular day certainly stands out. On 18th April 2017 we went on a 'family' twitch on our boat to Noss to see the hermit thrush which Craig Nisbet had found on the north-east side of the island. I will never forget having Ayda hand in hand whilst carrying my then rather cumbersome camera gear as we boarded the boat, with some nervous trepidation and anxiety, and later wading through a few feet of water to actually reach the island from our mooring spot. Another rare sight en route was to see Ayda in a baby carrier on Phil's back as we headed up purposefully along the cliff edges and the 20-minute walk to the thrush's last known location. We eventually enjoyed incredible views of the hermit thrush as it ascended from an obscured geo floor and rose up and up until it was out in front of us on the cliff top as we sat watching in awe. I am not sure how I managed any shots at all as I remember trying to curtail Ayda's loud chortles around the bird and other birders (though if anything they appeared to only encourage the thrush closer!) and keep her away from the cliff edges, but I succeeded and it was a welcome 'family' British tick. I remember being shattered after arriving home that evening, but elated at the same time as the anxiety finally started taking a back seat.

More recently, and I still find it unbelievable to write it, we had the good fortune of seeing and experiencing a number of times not one but two Tengmalm's owls in Shetland; a bird of pure birding gold status. The initial jaw-dropping news of a Tengmalm's owl at

Shetland Seabird Tours – The Noss Boat with Atlantic white-sided dolphins *(Lagenorhynchus acutus)*, Lerwick, August 2018, © John Coutts.

Tumblin in Shetland in February 2019 was met with disbelief and extreme upset for us, as we were actually with family in Suffolk when news broke – but both Phil and I managed to twitch Shetland separately, one after the other, to tick the 'mega' and then saw it again on our return to our Shetland home a while later. We were to play a part in the unfolding story of these two birds, as well as helping manage the massive invasion of visiting birders. Surely the bird(s) of the decade!

As the years roll on, so too does the increasing bank of memorable, super bird encounters and fine birding days in Shetland and Fair Isle as we continue to 'live the dream'. Though perhaps more than ever before, emphasis for us both has started to move away from purely personal gain and self-gratifying birding encounters to more conservation-based, educational, inspiring birding experiences both with our daughter and the many passengers we engage with whilst guiding boat bird tours.

Wryneck in Unst

29th August 2019
Julie Redpath

My first time doing a 'big year', in 2019, was filled with incredible experiences, highs and lows aplenty. But sharing the birding experience is a joy of which I never tire. And so it was that Phil Harris, also listing, heard of a wryneck up in the island of Unst, during August. The wryneck, which had been found at a favoured spot in Unst, was too good to miss. I arranged to meet Phil at the Halfway House, at Sandwater, and travel up with him. I figured it would increase our chances of finding such an expertly camouflaged bird if four eyes were looking. The journey up was smooth and uneventful.

The bird had chosen a ruined croft house surrounded by dense shrubbery and low trees: a relatively small plot to search through, flanked on both sides by inhabited croft houses and gardens. I think we did a thorough job of searching too. We scoured every inch, every bush, rock and wall – again and again. A couple of warblers and a flycatcher, that quickly vaporised, added nothing new to our year lists and was all we got for our efforts. The original finder, Dave 'super' Cooper, resident in Unst, came back to give us a hand, but couldn't rediscover the bird for us either. Eventually we gave up.

Along the road, back towards the ferry, we were stopped by a young fulmar, who had misguidedly landed on the road. Now the bird couldn't take off. So I jumped out, and carefully picked it up with the head far away from me. Unfortunately, it had scraped its feet which left blood splattered throughout Phil's cab and over me!

Our detour to release the bird back on the sea meant we passed by a female hitchhiker. We presumed she was heading for the campsite and so offered her a lift. I innocently explained to her: "It's okay, the blood splatters aren't ours!" Phil hooted with laughter, and the poor hitchhiker looked wide-eyed, before I realised what I had said. Hastily, I explained about the fulmar.

We safely made it onto the ferry, without having to explain to any policeman why we had blood all over the cab, for our return to Yell. Once the ramp was up, Phil's phone rang – it was Brydon Thomason. Lots of expletives followed, with Phil sliding out of the van door yelling, "We've got to get off!" at the deckhand. Amazingly, they did let us off and we drove back to Baltasound to look at a lovely dotterel (a lifer for me) and of course one for the list. Wow, that lifted our spirits! The journey home was much jollier after that. Thanks Brydon.

Phil dropped me off at my car, and I said, "See you later," (a bird club committee meeting was scheduled at Phil's home). Why couldn't I get into my car? Where were my keys? It turned out they were not with me. A hasty phone call to Phil – could he come back and get me? The bird club committee meeting was great, but my poor son had to retrieve my spare keys, pick me up from Lerwick and take me to my car. I was not popular!

I am well-known for losing things, but generally I don't worry as I know I will find them again. But losing my car keys bothered me, and stopped me from sleeping, as I hadn't long bought the car. Also, I wasn't sure when I had lost them. This added to the discomfort. In the morning off I went, first ferry of the day, back to Unst to look for them. Everywhere we had gone the previous day I searched: dotterel, wryneck, fulmar rescue and release site, hitchhiker pick-up and drop-off, and ferry terminal site, toilets and buildings. Nothing.

Brydon Thomason had a look for me, also without success. Back for a last look at the wryneck site before heading home, I bumped into Dave Cooper again. Whilst we were chatting, he casually quipped, "Oh, look at that, the wryneck!" And there it was, sitting on top of the ruin, gazing about, as only wrynecks can do, before flying off into the bushes. Cheekily, I put the sighting out on our bird news groups. Phil was not impressed when he read the news ... but the tick was great, despite the financial pain that losing my keys was going to be.

Some weeks later I received a phone call from Leask's garage in Lerwick, where I had bought my new car. It went something like this: "Mrs Redpath, you won't believe what has just happened. A tall, heavily-bearded man with a large rucksack has just walked down from Unst to get the NorthLink boat tonight, and has handed in your keys. He said he found them on a windowsill at Belmont ferry terminal." No words!

The result of the 'big year'? Sadly for me it was interrupted by family illness during the crucial month of October, but still I made a creditable 238. I also became the first woman on the unofficial league table of 'Shetland big years'.

Hawk owl in Mainland and Bressay

12-13th September and 20-21st September 1983

David Okill

It was just another day in the office. I was sitting at my desk working, when the phone rang. It was Dennis Coutts. He explained that he had just had a call from Angus Nicol, one of the residents at Frakkafield, a couple of miles north of Lerwick, to say that there was a hawk owl in the garden. Dennis seemed slightly sceptical and couldn't leave because of appointments. He suggested that I should check it out on my way home.

At 5 o'clock I picked up Gill and we headed home. Half way there I remembered the phone call; so we turned and drove back to Frakkafield. Identifying the right house, I was invited in and shown into the living room. On the far side of the room there was a picture window and beyond the window was a small bush. Sitting on top of the bush was a small owl, unblinking bright yellow eyes staring straight in at me.

What! It was difficult to say anything at that point but I asked to use the phone to phone Dennis (before the days of mobile phones). "Dennis, it is one." You could almost hear the scream of tyres as he left Lerwick. He arrived a few minutes later and was, of course, delighted. Another bird for the list.

After a while the bird flew a short distance across the golf course, to where there was a small patch of bushes surrounding an old derelict croft house. It sat on top of one of the tallest bushes, staring about. It was here that Dennis subsequently got some photographs.

We had put the word out and people started to arrive, getting great views of the bird from the main road without disturbing it. They were all well pleased. Generally it had brownish-grey plumage, the pale face was framed by dark lines, it had large pale shoulder patches, a finely-barred pale belly and a distinctive long tail. What a cracking bird!

It was there until dusk and still present briefly the following day, much to the delight of the early arrivals, but it disappeared soon after dawn. We presumed that was the last time we would see it. However, it was found again a week later at Gorie, Bressay, at an

Hawk owl *(Surnia ulula)*, Frakkafield, September 1983, © Dennis Coutts.

abandoned croft and was present the next day before finally leaving not to be seen again, despite some folk searching.

This bird coincided with a small influx of these owls into southern Scandinavia. At the time, it was the tenth British record (subject to review), and the second record for Shetland; the first was a bird at Skaw, Unst, during the 1860-61 winter, when it was collected.

Editorial comment: *Those who missed this bird at Frakkafield were fortunate to get another opportunity to see it in Bressay. Iain Robertson remembers that the miraculous second-coming in Bressay would probably have gone unreported had not an ex-Noss warden, Clare Dore, with Robin Wynde, decided to attend a Shetland Bird Club meeting in Lerwick and casually announced that they had a hawk owl in the garden! Iain spent the night on their floor, whilst Pete Ellis twitched it from Out Skerries.*

Following a review of British records of hawk owls by BOURC (Harrop 2010), only four were found to be acceptable. These included the records from Shetland in 1860 and 1983. The 1983 record occurred during an invasion of hawk owls, which brought large numbers to southern Norway and Sweden, 510 to Denmark and a single to Germany. An oral report from lighthouse workers in the Faeroe Islands in autumn 1983 has been published previously, but lack of details in the description led the Danish Records Committee to reject the observation (Silas Olofson in litt.). It is notable that there is just one accepted record from Helgoland (Dierschke et al. 2011), on 11th and 13th October 1974. The wait for another Shetland record continues.

The first British great knot

15th September 1989
Pete Ellis

Fifteenth September 1989 was a fine sunny day with a light easterly wind, so I went out for a quick look round South Mainland. Grutness had a good scatter of common migrants including blackcap, lesser whitethroat, a couple of garden warblers and a nice barred warbler, so where would I go next? I decided on Scatness and walked along from the main road, so I could check all the gardens on the way. There were fewer migrants there, but four whinchats were welcome.

As it was around high tide, I decided to walk further out along the peninsula to look for waders roosting on the short turf around the small pools there. I saw a small group of waders about 150m ahead, so I stopped near an old stone structure, which I could lean on to steady my binoculars while I checked them. There were three grey plovers, two dunlin, a knot and just beyond them another wader that looked really interesting. I leaned my telescope on the wall of the structure to get a better view, and couldn't believe my eyes. Its size, structure, striking black breast band and black mantle with a pale chestnut band across the lower scapulars told me it was an adult great knot in summer plumage. The knot nearby allowed for a close comparison with the new bird. I noted the longer more drooping bill, much longer wings, and the lines of heart-shaped black spots along the flanks. The breast and upperparts were more uniformly black than the illustrations and photographs I could remember, but it really was a great knot.

Suddenly, all the waders took off and I felt the onset of panic. Luckily, they flew towards me and landed at the edge of a small pool only about 60m away. The great knot's white rump and almost total lack of wing-bar were striking in flight. It began feeding again on the short turf, but after just a couple of minutes, a redshank flew close over it, flushed it and they flew off together, disappearing to the north. I checked Moast Beach, not far to the north, which is a good place for waders, but could not find it there.

I walked back to my car at the main road and drove to a phone box in Toab (this was before mobile phones) where I phoned Martin Heubeck. I told him that I had found a great knot, but asked him to bring the *Shorebirds* guide down to the phone box, as I wanted to

Great knot *(Calidris tenuirostris)*, Virkie, September 1989, © Dennis Coutts.

make certain that I hadn't remembered the features wrongly, before I took the plunge and put the word out on the local grapevine. About ten minutes later, Martin arrived with Paul Harvey. After one glance at the relevant plate in *Shorebirds* I was totally happy with my identification and Martin put the word out. However, at this point we had no idea where the bird was.

Paul and I went back to Scatness, but saw no sign of it. We thought and desperately hoped that, as the tide dropped, it would appear on the Pool of Virkie. Fortunately, after only about 15 minutes, Paul saw the bird feeding on the far side. What a relief!

Most of the local birders managed to get good views of it in the next hour or so. Dennis Coutts was the only one to get a decent photo (this was also before digital cameras). It remained on the pool until 15.40 when it flew off high to the north. Luckily for several visiting birders, it returned about an hour later and remained until 18.30 when it again flew off north with two curlew. So, we went off to the pub for a celebratory pint.

By the evening, the wind had increased to about force six, ahead of a front coming in, which brought south-westerly gales and rain for the next few days. About 30 birders flew into Shetland the following morning, but despite much searching it was never seen again.

Editorial comment: *The only subsequent Shetland record, in Unst from 30th May to 4th June 2019, was described by Conlin (2019).*

Fair Isle

2nd October 2016
Ciaran Hatsell

From 2014-2017 I was lucky enough to be an assistant warden at the mighty Fair Isle Bird Observatory. 'Dream job' doesn't even begin to cover how incredible it was to get to live and work on the magic isle for four seasons. Unimaginable birding, incredible community, spectacular scenery, countless memories: it holds the crown of my favourite place on earth. While every day was brilliant and there were countless highlights, 2nd October in 2016 is one that'll take some beating.

Early October in Fair Isle. Many thoughts spring to mind from that sentence. Bleak, storm-tossed, waterproofs, driving rain, ditch stomping, rarity hunting. But calm? Balmy? T-shirt weather? Not normally! A high pressure system was sitting over us and the residents of the world famous Fair Isle were basking in the autumn sun. Jimmy Stout was in his shortest red shorts, washing was out on the line at every croft, and the birders in the isle were bristling with anticipation.

The previous day had ended like any other autumn day in Fair Isle, a few drinks in the bar and a nightcap in the AW office discussing the prospect of rarities to come the next day. Reading old chatty logs over a few Tennents and a whisky, overlooked by a Barry Sheene photograph from his Man of the Year award, we sat speculating about what was to come. Weather charts open, this day in history read proudly aloud. This was the birding equivalent of Christmas!

The morning trap round had produced a couple of yellow-browed warblers and Mr Parnaby had caught a few common migrants in the Obs mist nets, in amongst them a gawky common rosefinch. Even small arrivals or a solitary scarcity in Fair Isle can be the harbinger of a good day; it really doesn't take much for the floodgates to open. It was enough to tickle the rare taste buds and after a quick brekkie, the army of rare-finding foot soldiers marched out from the Obs.

On the way out, the irrepressible Parnaby caught four yellow-browed warblers in the Gully alone, along with a few common migrants. This was the first inkling that today could be special. Whilst processing the lemon-and-lime phylloscs, a message came through that Kevin Kelly had found a Radde's warbler at Burkle. I think I heard an "Ooft!" from the nearby Andy Close as the small throng of assembled birders made their way down the isle to clap eyes on the peach-bummed-bruiser of a warbler. The call that a rarity had been found in the SE section of the isle was music to my ears. I knew that ahead of me and Andy

Denton (visiting from Noss) lay the untouched SW cliffs teeming with potential. My rarity-senses watering, we finished processing the sprites and marched on, clad in T-shirts and optimism, ready to cover every blade of grass, peer down every geo, scour the underside of every single nettle leaf in search of migrants.

The cliffs didn't disappoint. The first geo was packed full of yellow-browed warblers, their calls bouncing around the famous geos of Fair Isle's SW cliffs. Focus was needed not to double count and to try and look at overlap between sites. Aside from yellow-browed warblers there was a scattering of other migrants but it wasn't a huge thrush or finch fall, meaning there simply wasn't the sheer number of migrants to sift through. This was gonna be quality over quantity. Reaching the top of Hoini I got a call from Doddy, who had what he thought was a Blyth's reed warbler in the Haven. After a quick chat I basically told him that it was too rare to abandon census at the moment and he'd have to fly solo.

As we approached South Raeva, the first scarce migrant cocked its tail. A red-breasted flycatcher down on the rocks at the base of the geo was a welcome sight. Heading on to Steensi Geo, another red-breasted flycatcher was flitting around low down, fighting off the hordes of yellow-browed warblers for insects. The thigh-stretching climb of Malcolm's Head was rewarded when a third red-breasted flycatcher was found on the south facing slopes. A quick whizz back to double check they were different was a success, with all three birds still in situ. A hat-trick of RB flickers in such a small area was superb, but a wander down to Dog Geo would see it get even better ...

I have said many times in the past to Andy that we never find good birds whilst on census together. Whether this is linked to slightly decreased levels of concentration, a lessening of the 'spidey sense' of periphery, Denton being a curse or merely a coincidence, I don't know. As we approached Dog Geo, Andy split off to check out a rock he thought might have been something good. As I peered down into the cavernous, wet, black hole of Dog Geo, a movement caught my eye and, raising my bins, a cobalt bolt of colour flicked up onto the rockface. "Bluetail!" I shouted to Andy and we got great views as it flicked around the black rocks. The contrast of that shade of blue shining out of the gloom on a black cliff face was something I'll never forget. As was the imminent assemblage of bluetail admirers standing on the cliff top looking down in the sunshine. Iconic!

After a celebratory Twix, we marched on south. We met Parnaby and Steely who'd had pretty much nowt in SE but were chuffed there were birds coming in. Passing Midway and a happy Kevin Kelly, we got round to the back of Shirva when a piercing sound shattered the stillness. A grey wagtail-like "tsip tsip" call coming from a pipit descending directly overhead. It landed in Shirva garden and one quick bins view clocked the stripy mantle, primary projection and bubblegum legs. "Pechora!" I grabbed Andy and hugged him. This was a bird I'd dreamed of seeing in Fair Isle since I started, and one had got away from me the year before. After puncturing Andy's lung slightly we got the news out and waved like maniacs to anyone in the vicinity. While Andy kept an eye I popped in to see Stewart to see if it was okay for us to access his garden, and to tell him about the pipit. He said he was watching a programme about sharks on TV and gave us the nod to go into the garden, so I thanked him, gave him an Uncle Joe's mintball, and went on my way. Andrew Harrop eventually relocated the bird nearby which allowed many people to get point blank views – the happiness of a find only feels full when it's shared with those in the isle. Ridiculously, a red-throated pipit dropped in as a bonus for those looking for the Pechora: what a double!

It was genuinely hard to keep track of the new arrivals; an Arctic warbler was reported near Midway, barred warblers were popping up all over the place and mobile gangs of yellow-browed warblers were mobbing people as they went around the isle. Carrying on to

Pechora pipit *(Anthus gustavi)*, Fair Isle, October 2016, © Lee Gregory.

the shop we saw the Radde's warbler briefly and instead of returning to the Obs for lunch, we recircled back up to Pund and out to the SW cliffs again. There were still birds in the day. After battling our way through the clouds of yellow-browed warblers, news came through that a lanceolated warbler had been found at Midway, which eventually showed in classic Fair Isle fashion perched on the windowsill of an outhouse.

Despite birding from dawn 'til dusk and covering around 20 miles, there were no signs of fatigue or enthusiasm waning from the team.

The highlights of the final roll call at log were as follows:

> Pechora pipit: one at Shirva showed well at times, but was sometimes flighty; the 44th Fair Isle record (although with the most recent records falling in 2003, 2006, 2009 and 2012, this one was arguably a year late);
>
> Red-flanked bluetail: one in Dog Geo was the 13th Fair Isle record and showed well all afternoon on the dramatic cliffs;
>
> Lanceolated warbler: the fourth Fair Isle record of the year was found near Shirva before moving to Midway;
>
> Radde's warbler: one at Burkle proved mobile, but most people caught up with it;
>
> Red-throated pipit: one flew in calling before landing at Shirva, where it was seen briefly on the ground before heading off again;

Blyth's reed warbler: one in the Haven was later trapped when it moved to the Obs, although it then moved back to the South Haven where it fed on the beach for the afternoon;

Yellow-browed warbler: 72; marginally short of the Fair Isle record day count of 76 (set the previous year), but still an impressive sight;

Red-breasted flycatcher: 4; singles at Lower Stoneybrek and South Raeva and two on Malcolm's Head;

Barred warbler: 3; two at Stackhoull and a single at Burkle was an interesting late arrival;

Little bunting: one in Meadow Burn in the morning;

Common rosefinch: 3; one ringed in the morning at the Obs, with two unringed birds later at Burkle;

Bluethroat: 2; one still around Shirva and a new bird at Barkland;

Short-toed lark: favouring the Sheep Cru;

Siberian chiffchaff: 7; including one trapped and ringed.

The last abiding memory of that day's birding was of the sun setting at South Light and the calls of yellow-browed warblers echoing off the rocks as they bounced over the seaweed heading out to sea into the setting sun – pure magic! Although we might not have had a mega rarity, days like this filled with scarcities and scattered common migrants make birding one of the best things on the planet. Variety, anticipation, that feeling of a niche birding community grouping together in Britain's most remote inhabited isle for the shared purpose of finding migrants: bizarre and special in equal measure. Talking about it in the bar that night, many people declared it one of the best day's birding they'd ever had, including some senior stalwarts of the sport. It's one of those days that when each autumn comes around, birders who were there chime up: "Do you remember 2nd October 2016, super Sunday, on Fair Isle?"

Ovenbird in Out Skerries

7th October 1973
Iain Robertson

Many birders dream of finding a great rarity on their local patch but most never realise that dream, however sometimes luck is on your side.

Back in the day I was living in Out Skerries, working as a fish-filleter and undertaking a daily census of migrant birds on the islands. I had spent two seasons as an assistant warden at Fair Isle Bird Observatory and was employing the same daily census methods on Skerries, keeping a log of my sightings. In 1973 Skerries was very different from today. There was cultivation in the two main islands with rigs of oats, potatoes and turnips providing both cover and food for migrant birds; in addition there were many walled gardens full of cabbages and other vegetables. The islands were small enough for a single observer to cover most of the area in a day.

Seventh October 1973 was a Sunday so the fish factory was closed. I had done my rounds of the East Isle in the morning and in the afternoon I set out to do a circuit of the West Isle. There was a scattering of common migrants but no large numbers or any unusual species; just an average day. As I was walking beside the long stone dyke that runs down most of the West Isle I saw a totally unfamiliar bird run through a gap in the wall. It was about the size of a nightingale and with its tail cocked it had something of the jizz of that species, however it was bright olive-green above, white below with black streaks, and it showed a bright orange-tan crown bordered by black coronal stripes and a prominent white orbital ring. I crept up to the dyke and peered over to see the bird foraging for insects at the base of the wall about 10m from me. With better views I realised that I was looking at a North American passerine of the genus *Seiurus*. I had no experience of this group of birds but knew that two out of the three showed prominent supercila. This one didn't. I realised that I was looking at an ovenbird *Seiurus aurocapilla,* at the time placed in Category D of the British list on the strength of a single wing found on the tideline at Formby, Lancashire in 1969. (The taxonomy has changed since 1973 and ovenbird is now the sole member of the genus.)

It was very active, running about between the fallen stones at the base of the wall grabbing the odd morsel of food as it did so. Many months previously I had the foresight to stash a 20-foot mist-net and a couple of bamboo poles half-way along the dyke. Now was the time to deploy them. I set up the net through a gap in the wall and weighted the bottom shelf with stones. I took down a brief description of the bird in my notebook, then with my heart thumping, slowly walked it towards the net. It just ran at considerable speed under the bottom shelf. Fail! Undaunted I sneaked behind the wall and then crept up on the bird from the opposite direction; this time I waited till it was a few feet from the net, waved my arms and flushed it: success, it was in the net. I quickly extracted it, put it in a bird-bag, took down the net and went back to my house to process the bird. Duly weighed, measured, description taken and ringed, I took it outside for some photographs. By now it was late afternoon and the light was failing. I released the bird in a neighbour's cabbage patch hoping it would find both food and shelter there.

I was elated and desperately wanted to share my news: this was the first live ovenbird for Britain and indeed the Western Palearctic. At the time there were only a few birders in Shetland but I excitedly phoned the usual suspects to tell them of my find. There was no pub in Skerries, but if there had been …

The next day, Monday 8th October, a select crew of twitchers were due to arrive. Bobby Tulloch had sailed from Mid Yell in his boat to pick up Dennis Coutts from the Mainland and then Johnny Simpson from Whalsay. There were no ro-ro ferries in those days. I had spent the morning trying to relocate the bird without success. I went down to the pier to meet the boat and relate the sad news that I had been unable to find it again. With our spirits slightly dampened we all set off to the West Isle and to our considerable relief found the bird feeding on a grassy bank just above the shoreline. It flew off to a rocky hillside and continued to search for food. Good views were obtained and Johnny Simpson was so delighted that he waved his walking-stick in the air: that did the trick, the startled bird flew off never to be seen again – or so we thought.

I did not see the bird again despite searching for it during my daily rounds of the islands, but on 11th October a Whalsay fishing boat, the *Heather Bell*, spent the night at the Skerries pier. The following morning the skipper noticed an unusual-looking bird sheltering in a fish basket on the deck. On returning to Whalsay he mentioned his sighting to Johnny Simpson and perfectly described an ovenbird. The bird had left the boat off the coast of Fetlar.

In over 30 years of birding in Shetland I have had the good fortune to experience many memorable days in the field, from huge falls to iconic rarities such as great bustard and hawk owl, but finding the ovenbird has to be my best day.

Something to Yell about

Dougie Preston

Birding in Yell has given me some great days in the field and some fantastic memories. Even though the potential of my local island patch has been firmly proven many times over, it's still pretty much ignored by visiting birders, with most birders preferring to work the tried and trusted birding hotspots of Unst and South Mainland. I'd just like to add, if visiting birders can just keep this up, then it would be very much appreciated!

Now Yell is an island surrounded on most sides by other islands, and as such seems to miss out on a lot of the large migrant falls sometimes experienced by its neighbours. Periodically, when Whalsay/Unst/Fetlar are dripping with new arrivals, Yell can feel like an avian desert. Somehow good birds do still seem to find their way here, and sometimes very good birds too. It's possibly just not their first landfall in these islands, and they've perhaps filtered through.

During the autumn of 2017 I was doing some ecological survey work in the north of Yell, which involved many hours of watching vast areas of moorland from predetermined vantage points. The date in question was 18th October, and I'd just spent the last six hours seeing very few species in a particularly soul-destroying survey. Before heading home I decided to have a look over some of the various freshwater lochs nearby. Although most passerines have already abandoned the moorlands of Shetland at this time of year, wildfowl numbers are usually on the increase and are always well worth a look. Sand Water near Gutcher was the first place on my list to check.

Setting up my telescope to look out of the driver's window, a few minutes of scanning revealed common teal, Eurasian wigeon and tufted duck. It was then that a drab brown-looking duck caught my eye. It was fast asleep on the far edge of the loch, with its head completely hidden from view. I find trusting your instinct to be quite important when bird finding, and I'm still not sure what exactly drew my attention to this bird, but it was enough for me to set up my camera in the hope of getting a few distant digiscoped images, if it ever decided to raise its head. To my relief after a few minutes it duly cooperated, and revealed itself to be a first-winter male ring-necked duck. This was not only a nice 'self-find tick' for me personally, but also the first time the species had been recorded in Yell. Definitely a decent day!

Unbeknown to me things were about to get a whole lot better. It was while getting some distant photographs of the ring-necked duck, that another duck landed with a splash next to it. On a very quick first impression it appeared to be a juvenile velvet scoter. Immediately this drew my attention for a couple of reasons. The first reason was that in most years

White-winged scoter *(Melanitta deglandi)*, Unst, October 2017, © Jim Nicolson.

velvet scoter is a scarce bird in Shetland. The second reason was that unless they are breeding, scoters in Shetland are usually found on salt water, and this was a freshwater loch. I instinctively switched my attention to trying to obtain a couple of images (even though the bird was still some distance away). The scoter was constantly diving which made observing it quite difficult, and then after a few minutes it took off and headed in a roughly NE direction. However, one thing that I had already noticed through the camera viewfinder was the relatively straight bill profile, which is at odds with velvet scoter's usual concave bill profile. After I was sure the bird had indeed departed, I flicked through some of the images on the back of my camera. What was obvious from the less-than-perfect images was that the bill and head profile fitted the North American white-winged scoter *deglandi* far better than our own velvet. Other white-winged scoter features, like the feathering leading down the bill to the nostrils and forming a 90-degree angle, were also just about visible. What was undeniable was the raised nostrils, which were so pronounced that daylight could even be seen through them. This last feature is never found on velvet scoter, and is far more indicative of *deglandi* than 'Stejneger's' scoter.

It seemed obvious that the bird wasn't planning on returning to this loch anytime soon, and aware that lots of local birders would be interested to see it I started a methodical search of suitable nearby lochs. This was unsurprisingly unsuccessful as for a wayward sea duck Shetland has masses of far more suitable coastal habitat on offer.

I remember a quote by the late Martin Garner: "When preparation meets opportunity". And indeed it was Martin's own *Birding Frontiers* article written many years previously on identifying these species (although they were still only sub-species when it was written) that had stayed in the back of my brain till now and was the heads-up that this was indeed something very special. Due to the sheer rarity of white-winged scoter in Britain,

I was understandably starting to question myself. I decided the best course of action was to post an image on the local 'WhatsApp' sightings group. Almost immediately my phone was ringing and I was getting confirmation texts and calls from some highly respected birders and the bird information services. But best of all was a very positive response from one of the finders of the first record from Aberdeenshire in 2011. I sometimes forget how well the birding grapevine works when something good is found.

Thankfully for the Shetland listers, the white-winged scoter was re-found later the same day on another freshwater loch in the SW corner of Unst. It showed far better which allowed some truly stunning photos and videos to be taken over the next couple of days. Interestingly, what looks to be the same bird was also photographed on the sea off Unst a couple of days before my sighting, although the observers at the time never realised the bird's true identity.

To put the rarity of this sighting into context, a scoter photographed off Musselburgh on 26th December 2013 was accepted as either *deglandi* or 'Stejneger's', but was never officially accepted to species level. And there is compelling date and location evidence that all sightings on the east coast of Scotland possibly relate to just one individual, contrary to the BBRC's statistics (details recently sent to BBRC for consideration). Thus the Yell sighting is potentially only the second *deglandi* white-winged scoter for Britain.

Although I've managed to find some truly memorable birds in my home island of Yell over the years, I will always remember 18th October 2017 as one of my best birding days.

Shetland LadyBirders' mad dash to Unst for a Shetland first: White-winged scoter

21st October 2017
Julie Redpath on behalf of Shetland LadyBirders

Seven members of the Shetland LadyBirders (Lynne Hull, Mary Leask, Liz Holmes, Helen Perry, Julie Redpath, Linda Richardson and Denise Woodford) braved the near gale conditions for a chance of seeing a very rare sea duck. We ended up with one seat short in the minibus so Denise and Linda conceded that a second vehicle was the only way to go. Two vehicles headed northwards in 30mph south-easterly winds, with variable gusts, which made the journey all the more exciting. By the time we arrived at Gutcher, our last stop before landing on Unst, we had seen gannets fishing, herring gulls, lapwings, a fly-by merlin, starlings, house sparrow, wood pigeon, rock dove and grey heron. Stopping briefly at Sellafirth, we marvelled at the large roving flocks of redwing, blackbird and a jolly flock of brambling. Also in the fields were snipe – on the ground, and later clouds of them flying quickly past. At Gutcher itself, we added robin, goldcrest, great black-backed gull, fieldfare, red-breasted merganser and common gull.

Excitement building, as we drove off the ferry onto Unst soil, we headed straight for the Loch of Belmont and parked up by the nearby farm. With the wind pushing behind us, we headed down hill towards the loch. Wrapped in winter woolies, cheeks already rosy from the cold wind, my thoughts were: "Would the bird still be there? Had I dragged everyone out on a fool's errand?" It had already done a disappearing act after

LadyBirders, Dale of Walls, March 2019, © Julie Redpath

Dougie Preston had the briefest of looks at it back in Yell, before it was relocated on the Loch of Belmont. My heart was pounding. Would we be successful?

Whilst I was setting up the scope, Helen exclaimed, "Is that it?" I looked up and, sure enough, there it was! Everyone was able to get onto it with their binoculars, and had great views down the scope too, despite the increasingly inclement weather. This bird was a first for all those present. A first for the Shetland LadyBirders and a first for Shetland too.

Long-tailed duck, redshank, turnstone, hooded crow and teal were also present at Belmont, and so were added to the trip list. We made our way slowly to Easter Loch, between Uyeasound and Clivocast, to chance our luck with a ring-necked duck. Sadly, it wasn't there, but we did see newly arrived whooper swan families, lots of tufted duck, and reasonable numbers of goldeneye. A gathering of ravens caught our eye, along with the ever-present flocks of redwings. These birds compounded the feeling that winter had arrived.

Feeling the need for hot drinks and food, we headed to Last Checkout in Baltasound but not before another fly-by merlin was seen. Over lunch, it was great to spend a short while out of the wind, enjoying each other's company and finding out a bit more about each other's lives.

Heading down towards the shoreline at Buness, we encountered a tiny warbler in the bushes outside Baltasound Hotel. Helen and I tried to locate it but it didn't wish to be found. In the fields were amazing numbers of waders including golden plover, lapwing, snipe, dunlin (now sporting their winter plumage), and some mallard. Rock pipits flitted about on the road. Sadly, sea conditions did not improve our chances of seeing the surf scoter. In fact, we couldn't locate any birds in the voe.

After meeting a car filled with other intrepid birders, we stopped for a chat, before heading to the Halligarth plantation. With the increasing wind roaring through the trees, within the sheltered walled garden at Halligarth it was quite magical. Overhead, we heard the "seep" call of the redwings. Very few leaves remained on the old trees having already been blown off. Within the graveyard, Helen and I found a chiffchaff, and we were all completely enthralled by a mystery "ticking" call. Eventually, we had to concede that it was a tree branch squeaking in the gusty wind! A flock of bramblings and redpolls were seen by most of the group, although not well enough to see if any Arctic redpolls were hiding amongst them.

When we arrived at Setter Hill Estate trees, which had seen some lovely birds during the year, they were festooned with lovely, chatty, active goldcrests, always a favourite to see. As we drove away from Baltasound we saw more redwings, fieldfares, a couple of chaffinches, and some bright bramblings.

At the end of the day it wasn't the longest list to be sure, with 36 species seen. However, given the late autumn wintry weather it was not too bad, and the trip was really about that duck!

Background: Shetland LadyBirders began over the summer of 2016. Using Facebook as host, the group has steadily grown to 67 members (as of 25th May 2021). Julie Redpath leads the group and manages arrangements for meeting up and other events. Prior to Covid we had a monthly meet to bird together, often using a minibus if numbers allowed. Sometimes we would concentrate on a particular area, other trips it was types of birds. During migration times we went wherever the birds took us. During the winter months we focused on inside events, or nailing our winter gulls and ducks.

The only requirement to join is that you are female. I wanted to develop a group who could bird, laugh, learn and get out there in the male-dominated world that birding used to be. The group is a fabulous success. Members engage in breeding and wader surveys, we have taken part in tern and whimbrel national surveys, we engage with local birders to take part in bird races, and have run a few ourselves. We even made a quick appearance on BBC *Springwatch*. We have supported each other through the tough times that life throws at you, and have come out the other end, still going strong.

Women are now much more evident in all aspects of birding life, both in Shetland and elsewhere across the country. That is truly a great legacy to be part of.

The magic 23rd

23rd October 2013
Mike Pennington

The biggest element in finding a rare bird is surely luck. Perseverance, local knowledge, experience, identification skills – they all play a part–but at the end of the day you have to be in the right spot at the right time when the bird is showing. On 23rd October 2013, after being away for a few days, I decided to walk round Baltasound rather than drive to the north end of Unst. I decided to head towards the school instead of heading to Halligarth first as I would usually do and, after checking the lone tree in the Manse garden, I stopped for a chat and glanced across to the lone tree again, and this time noticed a strange-looking bird which definitely required a closer look. Such was the chain of fortune that led to the discovery of a second for the Western Palearctic.

I was chatting to another local birder, Dick Foyster, discussing the day's obvious arrival of thrushes and blackcaps, when I first saw the bird. From a distance the bird looked vaguely *Phylloscopus*-like, but it had a big pale patch on the wing. I suggested to Dick that we needed to have a closer look, so we strolled along the road towards the corner of the garden. The bird appeared again on the outside of the sycamore. Incredulously, I realised that this was something extremely interesting: "That's an American wood warbler!" The bird was on view for a good 20 seconds or so, long enough to realise what we were looking at and take in the most obvious features. This was, however, my best view of the bird for the next four hours.

Over the next hour the bird showed fleetingly in the lone sycamore. Dick had to leave as he had people coming to work at the house. My phone had no signal. My only attempts at taking a photo had captured some out of focus leaves. I could get very little more on the bird. Then it left the sycamore and headed to a small patch of nettles. By the time I got there, there was no sign of it. I returned to the sycamore: no sign. A bird flew past and I chased it: it was a blackcap. Two more blackcaps were chased down. It looked as though it had gone, and I still had no photos and only a cursory description.

I'd never been in this situation before, but faced with a *Setophaga* (they're not *Dendroica* any more), and one without obvious bright colours on it, my thoughts have always been start with blackpoll warbler and work from there. Some of the features seemed good for blackpoll: streaked underparts, fairly plain face, two wing bars, pale tertial fringes, white undertail coverts, some white in the tail. But the wing bars seemed odd; from a distance they looked more like a pale wing patch. And blackpoll tends to be a brighter bird, whereas this was a very dull greyish colour. There was something of yellow-rumped warbler in the plain face and streakiness, but there seemed to be no obvious yellow in the plumage (I hadn't seen the greenish rump or yellowish primary fringes at this stage). The bird *did* remind me of Cape May warbler, which I had seen in Cuba. But surely not; I knew that there was only one British record and that was in spring. It seemed that I might have something really, really good, but I still didn't have enough to be sure.

I decided to check the lone sycamore in the Manse garden once more before widening my search, and to my relief the bird had returned. This time I was determined to get photos as most views so far had been too brief to get any more detail than I already had. Eventually I grabbed a few poor photos in the worsening weather – it was definitely getting foggier all the time – before the bird left the sycamore and headed determinedly towards the old church at Hillside. The photos revealed one feature I had not yet seen in the field: a bright green neck patch.

At this point my wife Margaret arrived after Dick Foyster had phoned her. She brought two vital items: a copy of Sibley and a mobile phone on another network. I looked through the field guide. Could it be a really dull blackpoll with dark legs? Check the other species. Nothing fits. Except my long shot of Cape May warbler (there was that greenish neck patch on a dull greyish bird)! This was a big, big call and I really, really wanted someone else to see it. I was pretty sure it had to be a Cape May warbler, but it was massive leap of faith to actually believe it.

I phoned Brydon Thomason who was on his way back home to Unst but would not be back for over an hour. Then I phoned Paul Harvey and told him I had a *Dendroica* (yes, I know I should have said *Setophaga*!). As Paul was Shetland year-listing I knew he'd come even if it was 'only' a blackpoll, but I asked him how I would separate blackpoll from Cape May warbler. Mantle and leg colour were suggested. Dark legs and plain mantle pointed towards Cape May warbler again. We decided to put out news on the local grapevine, without a definitive identification for the moment, to give people the chance to come for it. I decided to try and relocate the bird and stay with it until help arrived.

Margaret and I headed down to the old church at Hillside where there is a small garden holding three sycamores. We saw the bird almost immediately, but it was as furtive as ever, mainly revealing itself when chasing off a chiffchaff and a blackcap that dared to enter the trees. Just before Brydon Thomason arrived, though, it started feeding off the walls around the small garden. This meant that Brydon got good views and more photos almost as soon as he got there. The bird even started calling in flight, a sharp "tsip", almost reminiscent of song thrush or a rare bunting. Brydon had also brought a copy of Kaufman and he too went through the process of elimination via the field guides. Conclusion, it had to be a Cape May warbler!

Now that it was conclusively identified, the bird suddenly decided to stop hiding and started feeding along the wall behind the sycamores. Whereas I had never seen it perched for more than a few seconds before, it now sat in full view on the wall. It was only now that I finally saw the bright greenish rump and the yellowish fringes to the remiges, but we could also see the greenish neck-patch, which was only visible at some angles, and the broad fringes to the greater coverts that produced the wing-panel that was so obvious at distance.

Paul Harvey and a few other observers arrived soon afterwards, and about 20 or so people made it up from mainland Shetland before dark. The next day more than 60 people saw the bird, with the highly novel sight of five aircraft parked together on the apron at Baltasound airstrip. By the end of the weekend (27th October) I estimate that at least 200 people had seen the bird.

Cape May warbler *(Setophaga tigrina)*, Unst, October 2013, © Rebecca Nason.

It was only after it went dark on the first evening that the enormity of the find sank in. This was not just a second for Britain, but it was only the second for the whole of the Western Palearctic. This is a species that had not even turned up in the Azores. This is a species that had never been found in autumn anywhere on this side of the Atlantic, the previous British record involving a singing male in spring, found by Tom Byars and Iain McDonald in Paisley Glen, near Glasgow, on 17th June 1977. It may not be a first for Britain, surely every rarity-finder's holy grail, but this was just as good in my eyes.

Ironically, this bird would have been on my local patch if I had got round to entering the Patchwork Challenge, but I never got myself organised. I had been keeping a list and thinking of joining "next year", but the Cape May warbler (and Brydon's Baltimore oriole from September) meant that "next year" might just have too much to live up to!

Memories from Fair Isle

Deryk Shaw

So, with over 20 years of living and birding in Fair Isle, 12 of them as warden of the Bird Observatory, choosing a best day's birding is difficult, there have been so many memorable days: I can still fondly remember my first Fair Isle rarity – a lesser yellowlegs on 1st May 1999 – although I can more distinctly recall the panting, sweaty assistant warden pounding his fists against the glass of my full-height living room window; back in the day before mobile phones he had run all the way back from Golden Water to deliver the news! Then, a couple of weeks later, the thrill of finding my first rarity as warden, a fine male rustic bunting in a ditch outside the Obs.

Or perhaps the day during my first winter when I had been tied to the computer, listening to the hail and sleet battering against the skylight all morning; a lull in the afternoon tempted me outside (not that I needed much tempting – I really had to stretch my legs, get some air) and I had reached the southern wall of the Auld Haa where I had stopped to shelter from yet another vicious shower. I scanned out to sea to count a flock of whooper swans flying past in the distance when my view was blocked by a different large white bird hanging in the wind over the cliff face at South Harbour: a gyr falcon. It immediately dropped out of sight so I raced to the edge, just in time to see it rise up again and hang just a few metres above my head for a few seconds before it drifted toward Skerryholm, immediately dived on a starling, then carried it off in one foot towards Malcolm's Head. What a bird! It remained on the isle for two weeks and I saw it every day, quite often just perched on a boulder halfway up Burrashield but I also witnessed it chasing starlings and pigeons and putting on an impressive aerobatic display as it chased off a pair of annoying ravens who were trying to steal its rabbit lunch.

A knock on my bedroom door by Alan Bull at 5am on 16th May 2003 with a request to see me in the Ringing Room (followed by the threatening 'whisper' from my wife of "Don't wake the children!") had me trooping bleary-eyed along the corridor, wondering what part of the Obs had catastrophically broken now. Opening the door, half expecting to see that the guests from the room above had crashed through the ceiling and were now (still in their pyjamas) sitting in their bed in the Ringing Room, I was surprised to find a grinning Glen Tyler standing there along with Alan who handed me a bird bag. I delved into it to feel a sizeable bird with a long tail, a shrike perhaps? I lifted it out in the ringer's grip: "Oh, nice, a great reed warbler!" I exclaimed.

"No!" said Alan. Suddenly I woke up. Adrenaline levels rocketed. The head was all wrong: it had to be a thick-billed warbler. In May? It can't be. Alan's and Glen's grins got even wider.

"Yep, I've measured it," said Alan. And it was a thick-billed warbler! Fair Isle's second and Shetland's (and Britain's) fourth record, but the first in spring. This sparked a major twitch to Fair Isle, the first I'd witnessed. The buzz was incredible. Excited twitchers arriving in tiny little planes, desperate to see the bird in what little time they had before their plane had to depart again. Thankfully, everyone who came was successful. But that buzz was nothing compared to the events of the autumn that followed.

September had been okay, with yellow-breasted bunting, multiple lanceolated warblers, Blyth's reed warblers, Arctic warbler, Arctic redpoll, stacks of yellow-browed warblers, and had ended with a Savi's warbler. Following a period of strong north-westerlies in early October, the wind switched to the fabled southeast on 13th October, resulting in a large fall of thrushes, blackcaps, goldcrests and finches with a fair smattering of scarcities (Richard's pipits, barred, Radde's, yellow-browed and Pallas's warblers).

Winds were still in the southeast on 14th October, so I headed out on SW census full of optimism, but by the time I'd got to the southwest corner of the isle, apart from hundreds of thrushes, the best I had seen was a yellow-browed warbler and the first woodcocks of the autumn. I then received a phone call reporting 'a funny little bunting' at Neder Taft and was asked if I could check it out. On arrival the only two people there, John Walmsley and Tony Quinn, both gave me similar descriptions: "It looks like a little bunting but doesn't have a chestnut face." The bird then appeared in front of us and it was indeed about little bunting sized but with streaks and stripes like no bunting I could recall. I informed my companions that I thought it was an American sparrow species but couldn't say which one. Shouts, waves and phone calls soon resulted in a crowd gathered at the Neder Taft garden, the Sibley guide was produced and Savannah sparrow seemed the most likely candidate, but our bird didn't seem to entirely fit the depiction: no yellow in the fore-supercilium, breast streaking appeared black not brown. The bird appeared settled in the garden and we had to get back to the Obs for lunch so we left John Walmsley to watch over it.

Consultations over lunch further strengthened the belief that it was a Savannah sparrow but I thought we'd perhaps need to trap it to be sure. Back on site, a net was erected and the gloomy, dull weather brightened up and, in better light, scope views and photographs indeed did show some yellow in the supercilium and the breast feathers were indeed black-centred, bordered with brown and with white fringes. Identification confirmed, I phoned Birdline Scotland and contemplated the arrival of twitchers that would follow. The bird then landed in front of the net and was quickly trapped, and once processed was released back at Neder Taft, sporting its shiny ring, where it remained until 19th October.

Now that was only half the story of that autumn as, on 17th October, Alan Bull found a female Siberian rubythroat; a discovery which actually hurts me a little as I had asked Alan to do my census that morning as I was seeing my parents off on the plane so couldn't do it. The elation that Alan felt that morning could have been mine! (I've now seen six rubythroats in Fair Isle but still never found one, although I did refind one that Nick Riddiford had seen in his garden late one evening and I spotted at Auld Haa two days later.) Still, this was my first and I was extremely happy about that. It certainly gave us the run-around and was very adept at flicking over a wall and disappearing only to be re-found an hour or two later several hundred metres away. Those few days will live long in the memory and resulted in (to date) Fair Isle's biggest ever twitch: over 150 people, with those arriving on 17th October to twitch the Savannah sparrow being informed that there were now two megas to look for: a lucky bonus for some but for others it meant two long trips north in just a few days. A few even travelled from Scillies to Fair Isle and back twice in that time!

Chestnut-eared bunting (*Embriza fucata*), Fair Isle, October 2004, © Rebecca Nason.

The following October (2004) was almost a repeat, just featuring different species, but started off with another presumed little bunting that "looked a bit odd" at the Skadan bird crop. First seen by Hywel Maggs on the morning of 15th October (he unfortunately had to depart that afternoon) I caught up with it late that afternoon and I, too, thought it wasn't right: too long-tailed, lacking black ear covert surround and it possibly may have had a chestnut rump but the light was fading fast so I decided (with no obvious other candidates to mind) that these were all apparitions of the poor viewing conditions. However, it was bugging me all night, so the following morning I asked assistant warden Rebecca Nason to keep an eye out for it on her census. She confirmed its presence, so after lunch a group of us headed down for more views. It still wasn't showing well but from what could be seen it clearly wasn't a little bunting yet didn't fit any bunting species we were aware of. I decided we should trap it.

Once in the hand, excitement levels rose as it did have a chestnut rump but clearly was something different from the other buntings with this feature that we were aware of (yellowhammer, pine, chestnut, yellow-breasted, rustic). Back in the Ringing Room and whilst I took a detailed description, my accomplices were researching books and journals and shouting out features/measurements for me to check. It was Phil Harris who eventually found the answer. He remembered an article by Steve Votier on vagrant eastern buntings in an edition of *Birding World* which he had recently been perusing, and went off to retrieve it. He quickly returned and slapped down a photo of our bird – a chestnut-eared bunting. References for this species were sought and features and measurements checked and confirmed that we had a first-winter male. Steve's caption underneath his photo was priceless: "Chestnut-eared Buntings breed in northeast China and Korea and are middle to long-distance migrants to their wintering grounds in southeast Asia. This

Siberian thrush *(Geokichla sibirica)*, Fair Isle, September 2008, © Deryk Shaw, "As I arrived at the gully ... a song thrush dived down past a 'blackbird': a 'blackbird' which then turned its head sideways ... and showed off a massive white supercilium!"

species has not been recorded in western Europe but a bit of blind optimism never hurts!" Wow! We had a first for the Western Palearctic!

It remained faithful to the Skadan crop until 20th October, allowing 120 or so birders to make the trip to see it. Three days after its departure, FIBO director Mike Wood was strolling along the road past Bull's Park with his wife and two small children when he spied a small chat-like bird hopping along the roadside. Mark Newell was nearby so he called him over and together they watched the bird and came to the conclusion that it was a *Catharus* thrush. I had just reached the top of Ward Hill when I received the call and probably broke the speed record for descending the hill and sprinting to the airstrip. By the time I arrived it had been identified as a veery, but nobody was entirely sure. I thought its colouration was more like hermit thrush, although the breast pattern was indeed closer to veery, so put the news out nationally as a possible hermit thrush. Discussions continued over lunch and it was Nick Dymond who mentioned that it looked a bit like rufous-tailed robin, a species he had encountered on his trips to Asia. Yet again, books were delved into and the internet scoured and I was staring in disbelief at an image on my computer screen when Alan Bull burst in with a similar photo in a copy of *Birding World*. Wow! We had *another* first for the Western Palearctic! Happy times. I phoned Paul Harvey, who was part of a boatload of Shetland birders hoping to see a hermit thrush, to pass on the news. Unfortunately the signal was very weak but I think he got the message. Apart from those already present, they were the lucky few to also see it as, following a clear night, it had departed by the next day.

The excitement of being involved in the identification of firsts for the country (or Europe even) certainly gives one immense satisfaction and a certain buzz, but finding your own special birds is even better. Spring 2008 had been special for birds with four additions to the island list, including Britain's first citril finch, but the quality of birding in the autumn was outstanding. I was on north census on 24th September and had reached the west side of Ward Hill and was making the ascent to the top, with multiple yellow-browed warblers flitting ahead of me, when I spied a bird fly-catching at the ruins at the top. It looked like a dumpy flycatcher, which puzzled me, but I thought I'd catch up with it in a minute or two; however when I arrived there was no sign, just the 10+ yellow-browed warblers. Making my way down the other side I once again caught a brief sight of it at the building half way down and noted a grey face and black beady eye with a white eye-ring before it flicked round the corner. As it did so I expected to see the tail pattern of red-breasted flycatcher, but no, it was plain grey like the rest of the bird. This got me thinking that it may have been a brown flycatcher, but once again it had disappeared. A few more yellow-browed warblers later and I'd reached the mast where I finally got a decent view of the bird and was delighted to confirm my suspicions. Wow! What a thrill! Thankfully the bird remained around the mast all day, allowing 40 or so people to see it.

There were twitchers at Tingwall waiting for news the following morning so I headed up to check the area but after searching at the mast, Ward Hill and the peat cuttings to no avail, I went round to Guidicum. As I arrived at the gully at the top, a song thrush dived down past a 'blackbird': a 'blackbird' which then turned its head sideways to look up and showed off a massive white supercilium. "Oh, my God, it's a male Sibe thrush!" I yelled internally to myself. That is one species on everyone's dream finds list. Everyone got to see it that day, even those who were waiting at Tingwall for news of the brown flycatcher, as it barely moved 20 feet all day, content scrubbing around in the moss and grass in the gully. It gave me great pleasure to be sitting at the top of Guidicum later that afternoon in beautiful calm conditions alongside Paul Harvey and Roger Riddington watching this enigmatic bird: a great end to a great (couple of) day's birding.

The 'big year' 2013: an attempt at a record Shetland year list

Paul Harvey

Choosing a best day in Shetland is an impossible task; there are just so many memorable experiences. Sitting on a boulder beach amidst the near-deafening noise of densely-packed guillemots, interrupted only by the guttural croaks and hisses of nearby shags, an adult razorbill standing on my left foot watching me anxiously, as I carefully ring its 14-day-old chick. Early mornings surveying blanket bog in the company of trilling dunlin, bubbling whimbrel, the haunting calls of golden plover and the crazed, cackling and barking of displaying red-throated divers. Drifting slowly through a flock of a 1,000 long-tailed ducks on a calm winter's day as they noisily display to each other in some kind of pre-migratory courtship ritual. Then there is the unpredictability of Shetland; where else could you see a beluga, a bundle of pink blubber morph into a tusked walrus, a breaching humpback or be so close to orcas that the spray from the blowhole literally lands on your forehead! For me though, I guess it's the thrill of finding rare migrants that is perhaps the single biggest driver and, rather than a day, I want to focus on a year. A so-called 'big year'.

The origins of year-listing in Shetland go back over 30 years. Dave Suddaby was the first to make a concerted effort to see as many species as possible in Shetland in a year in 1990, when he set the bar at 219. Two years later, in 1992, Hugh Harrop revised the record upwards to 222, a mark that stood for nearly a decade before I had a go at it in 2001, finishing that year with a total of 231. Just four years later, Steve Minton blew that total away, with a new record of 244 species in 2005.

Many folk have said: "Year-listing, why bother? What a waste of time!" Now, I am certainly not going to argue that the pursuit of a year-list has any great virtue, but just like running a marathon, or playing a round of golf, it does provide a personal challenge, and it has the added bonus of encouraging you to get out in the field at every opportunity. I'd always fancied having a go at beating Steve Minton's total but knew that I could only get close with the right set of circumstances. And 2013 seemed to provide the opportunity. I had retired after nine years of coaching the Ness U/14 football team, freeing up my evenings, and had a huge amount of breeding-bird survey work to do. Lots of early starts meant lots of time off in lieu. So, the scene was set.

January was all about connecting with a few over-wintering goodies. A smew at Clickimin on 2nd and waxwing in Lerwick on 3rd were good but, unfortunately, I was walking Muckle Roe with friends when Helen Moncrieff found a grey phalarope in Garth's Voe on 5th. I was on site at dawn next day but it had done a bunk: not the most auspicious of starts to a year-list. So, instead, I headed off to Whalsay to see John Lowrie Irvine's splendid drake king eider. Velvet scoter, brent goose, and a fine roast dinner, courtesy of John Lowrie and Angela, were unexpected bonuses. Great tit, blue tit and great spotted woodpecker, all remaining from the influx in autumn 2012, were nailed in Lerwick and Scalloway over the next week: all of them surpassed by Russ Haywood's big beast of a ring-billed gull at the East Voe of Scalloway on 16th.

I then set off to Ghana for a fortnight, managing to miss the only black-throated diver of the year. And then news of a pine grosbeak at Collafirth filtered through to West Africa! My mind was made up; should I miss the grosbeak then I would kiss the year list goodbye. Happily, the grosbeak stayed long enough for me to catch up with it, but the rest of February was hard going. A great crested grebe in St Ninian's Bay and a hen harrier in Bressay were the only birds of note as I wasted endless hours chasing a white-tailed eagle, all to no avail. With a total of just 98 at the end of February I was some way off the pace set by Steve Minton who had managed 113 in the same time frame back in 2005. March provided little fare to help close the gap, although Gary Bell's mistle thrush at Sumburgh on 18th and a marsh harrier at Brow Marsh on 31st were both species that could easily be missed.

Tystie surveying in Fetlar dominated early April. Mick Mellor's gyr falcon along the Fetlar banks remained a single-observer record but I did manage to catch up with a rough-legged buzzard there after 20 hours of scouring. Regular migrants were now starting to appear, but a coal tit found by Steven Flaws at Hestingott on 18th was a major bonus. Hugh Harrop found me a yellowhammer at Maywick on 21st yet by the month's end I was on just 128 species, 21 adrift of Steve Minton's total at the same stage.

May did not disappoint. A planned family weekend in Fair Isle produced a hatful of migrants, the best of which were pectoral sandpiper and stonechat. Hawfinch and garganey awaited my return on Mainland on 6th and a super male red-breasted flycatcher fed at Grutness on 8th. Another flycatcher, this time a stunning male collared found by Brian Marshall at Skaw in Whalsay, was the first real goodie of the spring on 10th. The 11th was one of those days when I really questioned my sanity. Robbie Brookes had tree sparrows on his feeders, but did I really want to go to Baltasound just for tree sparrows? The golden rule of year-listing is to take what is on offer, so off I went. The trip was successful, but I was to see several more tree sparrows closer to home before the year was out.

Seawatching at Watsness produced Manx shearwater and four pomarine skuas, all with a full set of cutlery, on 13th. The 16th was a proper red-letter day. Scotland's first Pacific diver was in Grutness Voe that evening and I wonder if I would have been there to find it if it wasn't for year-listing? Cuckoo, stock dove and wryneck were a good haul at Quendale on 18th, while first Roger Riddington (American wigeon) and then Ken Shaw (green-winged teal) provided me with American ducks at Hillwell on 19th and 20th respectively. North-westerly winds saw me back at Watsness on 21st when not one but 68 long-tailed skuas eased gracefully by, with their long tails bouncing along behind them, and a red-necked phalarope was an unexpected bonus. Julie Redpath kindly directed me to a first-summer little gull at Loch of Tingwall on the journey home.

Pacific diver *(Gavia pacifica)*, Grutness, May 2013, © Roger Riddington.

Red-flanked bluetail (*Tarsiger cyanurus*), Voe, October 2013, © Larry Dalziel.

Short-eared owl, icterine warbler, short-toed lark and quail were all useful additions at the south end between 22nd and 26th. David Parnaby had kindly been keeping me abreast of Fair Isle news, so I headed there for a few days on 27th to see his Blyth's reed warbler. Marsh warbler and bluethroat were soon added, and I managed to find myself three very useful year ticks: honey buzzard, hobby and thrush nightingale. So, at the end of May it was game on, I was just three shy of Steve Minton's total.

June proved to be a key month. The evening of the 1st was warm and sunny, and I was at Quendale enjoying Martin Garner's singing greenish warbler when Mike Pennington phoned up. He'd just found a woodchat shrike at Baltasound. So, head north it was and a few hours later I had connected with the woodchat; a good decision as it departed overnight. I also managed to catch up with a crane that had eluded me on previous visits, even though it was only 'on-foot' having sustained an injury to its wing. Jon Dunn's contribution of a drake ring-necked duck at Tingwall on 3rd was very welcome as I had almost given up on that species. Far more unexpected though was a phone call from SNH next day: "Stone curlew reported on Bressay," was the message. Juan Brown and I duly headed over at lunchtime but our initial search seemed to confirm our suspicions that it was nonsense. We were on the point of leaving, when it flew up and added some real quality to what was proving to be a good month. Fog prevented me getting to Fair Isle on 6th. It cleared the following day but unfortunately took the river warbler with it, meaning I had to settle for a (western) subalpine warbler and Temminck's stint. Phil Harris and Rebecca Nason directed me to a singing golden oriole at Kergord on 9th and a brief stop at Hillwell on the way to watch a football match on 11th provided a fine surprise in the shape of a drake black duck. Howard Towll's osprey at Brouster was a long shot on the evening of the 12th: they don't normally hang around and I had already missed several. The poor visibility meant it was worth a shot though, and yet another decision paid off – it sat on the same fence post for several hours. Iain Robertson's red-rumped swallow at Asta Loch kept up the pace and an unseasonal little stint was the last new bird of the spring on the 14th. All of which meant that by the end of June the total stood at 199.

July was poor until a blistering last week. A ruff kicked off proceedings gently enough on 24th and then on the 27th as I was debating whether to head up to Unst for two-barred crossbill, Rory Tallack found a small flock at Tresta. As we were enjoying them Steve Minton phoned to say he'd found a gull-billed tern at Scatness. Honourable, given that it was his record I was chasing. I sped south with Phil Harris, driving straight past a pod of orcas at Levenwick: they would have to wait until later. The tern performed and we then headed up to Lamba Ness in Unst to lure some petrels, trapping no fewer than six Leach's. The following evening a check through a large tern flock at Virkie revealed a stunning roseate tern. Another much-wanted Shetland tick, and the second new tern in a week.

Spotted redshank and rose-coloured starling were added in early August and then my attention switched to Fair Isle. A Swinhoe's storm petrel had been (re)trapped on several evenings and the weather on 12th looked suitable for petrel ringing. The petrel did not disappoint: and what a stunner it was, a species that I certainly never expected to see in Shetland. An early citrine wagtail on the isle was a bonus. Back on Mainland, seawatching at Sumburgh eventually paid off with a sooty shearwater close inshore on 17th. A barred warbler followed soon afterwards while George Petrie's wood warbler proved to be the only one I saw all year. On the morning of 18th August, I was greeted at Baltasound by Mike Pennington in his pyjamas! Rather than seeing his Mediterranean gull I had succeeded only in finding a roadside ditch and gone to his house for help. Fortunately, Larry Dalziel and Robbie Brookes, both of them fully clothed, were on hand and managed to ease my car out. The Med gull eventually appeared, making all the effort worthwhile. Symbister was my next port of call, this for a booted warbler on 29th, and then on 30th Ewen Thomson found a corncrake at Channerwick. Figuring this was probably my last realistic shot at this species I tramped around in the pouring rain for an hour before much to my relief I found it in an iris bed.

The first two weeks of September were dominated by westerly winds and I was beginning to feel despondent. Hugh Harrop and Roger Riddington lifted my mood temporarily by finding rare phylloscs in their gardens in the South Mainland: Arctic warbler and western Bonelli's warbler respectively. Then it was a long wait until Rob Fray's lesser yellowlegs at Virkie on 16th, and late in the day Mark Chapman phoned: "Dotterel at Eshaness." I had just over an hour of light, the evening meal I had just sat down to would have to wait. After a brisk drive I was delighted to clap my eyes on those big broad supercilia meeting on the nape as the bird crouched low among a flock of golden plovers. Much of the 19th proved extremely frustrating, scouring Baltasound for a Baltimore oriole found at Halligarth by Brydon Thomason earlier in the day. After several hours, convinced it was gone, I was on auto-pilot when, bingo! – it popped up in front of me in a small garden near the care centre. We even managed to get back down to Fleck to see Mick Mellor's American golden plover in the dusk. The Sandwick duo of Juan Brown and Glen Tyler found a monster snowball of an Arctic redpoll at Hoswick on 22nd, followed by olive-backed pipit and ortolan bunting in the next couple of days. Then it was into Fair Isle to see a Sykes's warbler, a trip which also produced a totally unexpected bonus in the form of a nightjar.

Some of our visiting birders in autumn work tirelessly in their quest for rarities and it was two such that were responsible for my next year-ticks, on 27th. Dan Pointon and friends unearthed a brown shrike at Wester Quarff before Pierre-Andre Crochet scored a Pechora pipit at Levenwick. Shetland was beginning to feel a little like Siberia. Yet, in typical fashion it was a rare yank that was next in the notebook when tour leader Dave Pullan phoned on 30th to say he had a Hudsonian whimbrel at Mid Yell. How lucky was

I, already sat on the Yell ferry! Good job too because it didn't stay long. So, as September closed, I was on 231, surely a half-decent October would yield the remaining 14 runs required.

On 4th October, I was en route to Yell for a hoopoe, when Dave Fairhurst found Britain's fifth thick-billed warbler at Geosetter. After a prompt u-turn I arrived to witness the biggest crowd I'd seen in the islands since Shetland beat Guernsey 2-0 in the final of the Island Games football! Luckily, I was standing in just the right place when the warbler made a rare appearance. It was back to Hoswick on 5th where Juan Brown and Pete Ellis had identified an eastern olivaceous warbler, but the next few days were to prove very frustrating. A third attempt at a great grey shrike in Bressay ended in another failure, but to make matters worse the Bressay ferry broke down (the second SIC ferry breakdown I'd experienced during the year) meaning I couldn't get to Mid Yell for Dougie Preston's buff-bellied pipit. The 8th was much better. A Richard's pipit at Virkie was followed by a great grey shrike at Cunningsburgh and then a rustic bunting in Fetlar. Visiting birder Graham Smith lined up a nice Wilson's phalarope at Sand on 9th and a day trip to Foula on 11th paid off with isabelline shrike and buff-bellied pipit. Big thanks to Geoff and Donna Atherton, Kris Gibb and Mark Wilkinson for those two.

Brydon Thomason cemented his place in my book of heroes on 12th when he found a paddyfield warbler at Skaw and a dipper at nearby Hermaness. A long drive and a long walk saw me within four of the record. A bullfinch and white-rumped sandpiper both played hard to get before eventually revealing themselves at Hoswick on 17th and Boddam on 18th. Then Brian Marshall found yet another goodie: a treecreeper at Symbister. Details of a red-flanked bluetail at Voe on 20th were sketchy but it was eventually located, and how fitting that this once mythical Sibe was the record-breaker; now 250 had to be a realistic milestone.

Poor weather foiled repeated attempts to get to Fair Isle to see a Siberian rubythroat but this proved to be a blessing in disguise as next up was arguably *the* bird of the year: Mike Pennington's Cape May warbler at Baltasound on 23rd. This was just the second British record of this American warbler. Next day it was back to Whalsay in the company of Howard Towll for sumptuous views of a juvenile Sabine's gull found at Skaw by Brian Marshall (again). We only just made it, the bird disappearing as we walked back to the car. Little auk was finally banked on 26th and later that day a tiny sprite of a Pallas' warbler entertained us in Trondra, although both shorelark and dusky warbler eluded me. I did manage to catch up with the latter at Helendale on the 28th: number 250!

November opened with Chris Rodger's flock of stunning white-headed long-tailed tits at Halligarth late on 3rd. Expecting these to move quickly I plumped to travel up that night. This proved a sound decision as two birds remained at dawn but left before anyone from the Mainland arrived. Missing Rebecca Nason's black-throated thrush at Gulberwick by just a few minutes on 9th was deeply frustrating, but amazingly she managed to relocate it at nearby Sound where it was enjoyed by all. And so, the regular wintering white-billed diver in South Nesting Bay on 13th proved to be the last species of the year: number 253, although in the fullness of time the eastern subalpine warbler at Mid Yell in late September will be split to bring the total to 254. What a year. So much time spent in the field seeing an awful lot of fantastic birds, largely thanks to a superb set of local and visiting birders.

Editorial comment: *Records are there to be broken and, in 2021, Phil Harris set a new record by seeing 260 species in Shetland during the year.*

Yell Sound and Sullom Voe

28th November 1978
Martin Heubeck and Mike G. Richardson

When asked to contribute to this book we had to think a bit because we'd never much been into spending a whole day out birding. We'd stumbled across some goodies while doing fieldwork (Ross's and ivory gulls, and a few Brunnich's guillemots) but nothing one could really base a whole day's account around. So we thought we'd go back to November 1978, and a timely day of early fieldwork. But first some background.

Mike came to Shetland in 1975 to take over as the Nature Conservancy Council's North Isles representative. This was at the height of the planning and construction phases of the Sullom Voe Oil Terminal, and he quickly became involved in the early seabird surveys, especially those in winter, and in the environmental monitoring plans that were being developed. In 1977, Professor George Dunnet, head of Zoology at Aberdeen University, became the chairman of the Shetland Oil Terminal Environmental Advisory Group (SOTEAG), on which Bobby Tulloch represented the Shetland Bird Club in his capacity as honorary president and general all-round naturalist. George Dunnet had been Martin's honours supervisor at Aberdeen, and in March 1978 asked him if he wanted to go to Shetland for a year to count seabirds for SOTEAG's fledgling monitoring programme. Having already done some summer seabird fieldwork in Shetland, when he'd met Mike and Bobby, Martin obviously jumped at the opportunity.

Mike and Pete Kinnear had spent a lot of time in the winters of 1975/76 and 1976/77 counting seabirds around Shetland, but especially focussing on Yell Sound and Sullom Voe, and the Bluemull and Colgrave Sound area between Yell, Fetlar and Unst, which was to be designated an anchorage for tankers waiting to enter the port of Sullom Voe. Some counts were from land, but many were made from Bobby's wooden boat MV *Consort*. From these counts a standard route was devised for each inshore area that would include as much of the seabird interest as possible within a single day, and within the twin constraints of the rather sedate speed of the *Consort* and mid-winter daylight.

So that's why we were standing at Ulsta, the inter-island ferry terminal in SW Yell on 28th November 1978, a calm, generally sunny day, watching the *Consort* approach on the

Bobby Tulloch and *Consort*, Fetlar, 1970s, © Jonathan Wills.

final stretch from Bobby's home base at Mid Yell. We'd already done the first 'standard route' survey of Bluemull and Colgrave Sounds on 21st October, with notable counts of 54 great northern divers and 5,867 eiders, and were keen to get a baseline count in along the Yell Sound and Sullom Voe route, not least because the first oil had been delivered to the terminal via the Brent pipeline three days earlier.

We set off from Ulsta at 10am heading north between the west coast of Yell and the islands of Bigga and Uynarey, and soon had the first of four little auks seen during the day. This was a perky, upright bird quite in its element and unlike the hunched, drooping-winged individuals that get photographed in harbours. The first three great northern divers were between the islands of Brother Isle and Little Roe, with 75 shags roosting on the tiny rock of Tinga Skerry (we counted cormorants and shags roosting ashore separately from those on the water or flying). Entering the 12km long Sullom Voe, we planned to follow the shore in a clockwise circuit, south down the east side and north up the west. There were another couple of great northern divers north of the tanker jetties, where the *Donovania* lay berthed and preparing to load and leave with the first ever shipment of crude from what would soon become Europe's largest oil-exporting terminal. Little did we know that the next time we'd be in the jetty area we'd be inspecting a huge gash in the hull of the tanker *Esso Bernicia*, with booms out trying to contain the 1,174 tonnes of heavy bunker fuel oil that had been released.

We continued into Garths and Scatsta Voes, and past the US Coastguard Loran station, encountering a good mix of eiders, long-tailed duck, goldeneye, red-breasted mergansers and Slavonian grebes in these shallower waters. The water is deeper further down the east side of the voe, with usually just a few goldeneye and red-breasted mergansers tight in against the shore. However, one should still look carefully for, in January 1987, we had just gone past a small duck sitting in the black shadow of the banks, which Martin and Nick Dymond were about to log as a goldeneye before yelling, "Stop!" to Bobby, and bingo, there was a harlequin duck! It prompted a considerable twitch.

Back to 1978: we turned at the head of the voe and returned up the shallower west side, again recording good numbers of duck, as well as 11 Slavonian grebes. The counts confirmed those of earlier surveys, generally made in less calm conditions, that in a Shetland context Sullom Voe hosted a good variety of divers, grebes and seaduck. The scatter of long-tailed ducks totalled 85, the last time they'd be recorded in double figures in the voe apart from 14 in February 1991, 20 in February 1993, and 13 in December 2019. We were also the last people to see a double-figure flock of velvet scoters in Shetland (16 in the northwest sector of the voe), a species that had probably been in long-term decline before the oil spill.

Leaving Sullom Voe, we crossed neighbouring Orka Voe scoring 10 great northern divers, 75 eiders and 90 tysties, before turning into Yell Sound again to start the run south between the Mainland coast and the islands of Bigga, Samphrey and Linga. For those who participated in subsequent surveys, that we had another 13 great northerns along this stretch might come as a surprise, but this was Yell Sound pre-oil spill. Passing the south end of Linga and heading east towards Lunna Ness we recorded another 18 great northerns, but also spotted a fairly tight group of five divers which on closer inspection proved to be black-throated divers, the most ever seen together in Shetland; three of these would later be found oiled and dead on the south coast of Yell. The light was fading as we turned off Lunna Ness and headed NNW over the shallow baa where 87 long-tailed duck and 114 eiders were still feeding, before crossing the deeper waters and swift tides of the south entrance to Yell Sound and arriving back at Ulsta.

Bobby still had the two-hour journey back to Mid Yell ahead of him, in the pitch dark with only a compass and his experience to guide him (no radar in those days); he would then bill SOTEAG the princely sum of £25 for the whole day! We took the ferry back to Toft quite pleased with ourselves and with the day's work. For Mike, it was satisfying that standardised monitoring of wintering seaduck and seabirds had begun, after the preparatory work several winters earlier. Martin, who was only 23 at the time and on a one-year contract, couldn't quite believe he was actually getting paid to do this stuff.

The *Esso Bernicia* oil spill, which happened around midnight on 30th/31st December 1978, devastated the seabirds present in Yell Sound and Sullom Voe at the time, and had a wider impact elsewhere in Shetland, with oil reaching north Unst, Out Skerries, Whalsay and Bressay. We repeated the November 1978 survey on 23rd January 1979 (*Table 2*), when most birds seen were cormorants and shags, which are highly mobile and normally spend a portion of the day roosting ashore. Counts for the other species speak for themselves.

Table 2. Counts of selected species, and for all diving seabirds and seaduck, on the surveys either side of the December 1978 *Esso Bernicia* oil spill (brackets = oiled but alive).

SPECIES	28/11/78	23/1/79
Eider	561	42
Long-tailed duck	214	16 (1)
Cormorant	55	57 (2)
Shag	620	230 (3)
Slavonian grebe	13	0
Great northern diver	53	2
Tystie	486	38 (4)
Total diving seabirds/seaduck	2,103	468

***Dunter III*, Yell Sound, January 2014, © Jonathan Wills.**

Counts along the standard survey route continued after 1978/79, albeit with some evolution, but describing changes in numbers of the different species over a 40-year period is a story best told elsewhere. Although very seaworthy, the *Consort* did have an unfortunate habit of developing temporary engine failure in just the wrong place at just the wrong time, and it was with some relief that Bobby replaced her with the *Starna* in 1987. Mike left Shetland in December 1989 for a post at the Foreign and Commonwealth Office's Polar Regions Section, but retained connections with Shetland and after retiring from the FCO chaired SOTEAG during 2010-2015. Bobby Tulloch's last Yell Sound trip was in October 1993, after which ill health took over and he died in May 1996.

The surveys went into limbo for a few winters until Jonathan Wills came to the rescue in January 1997 with MV *Dunter*, succeeded by *Dunters II and III*. Critics might say that one cannot compare the counts of three observers, sitting on comfortable swivel chairs high above the water on the flying bridge of *Dunter III* and equipped with very expensive modern binoculars, with those of the authors in 1978/79, braced against the wheelhouse of the *Consort* each clutching a pair of £70 10x50 Jenoptems. Probably not, but so long as the difference is acknowledged the data set holds good. The last Yell Sound run for *Dunter III* was on 29th December 2017, one day short of the 39th 'anniversary' of the *Esso Bernicia* oil spill. It was also Martin's last run in Yell Sound before retiring in March 2018, with Will Miles now continuing the SOTEAG counts using MV *Seabird*.

Birding Bluemull

Brydon Thomason

There are many elements that make time with Shetland's birds so special. The diversity of species the islands host throughout the year is truly unique, with a timeless relationship and rhythm between landscapes, species and seasons. More than even the weather, it has long been the birds that herald the season ahead. Be it the first song of a 'laverock', the evocative calls of 'rain gös', the first 'tirriks' of the year or the autumn return of the 'calloo', I learned this long before I ever lifted a pair of binoculars.

But what makes for the 'best day's birding'? It's not so long ago that if asked this, my mind would automatically begin a slide show of rarities found on unforgettable spring, autumn and even unexpected winter days and I am thankful there have been many great birds since I began birding over 30 years ago, growing up in Fetlar.

Over the years though, I have grown to appreciate that the days that mean the most are about so much more than the rarities. Just being with birds can be infinitely more special. Never more so for me than photographic assignments on species that have felt special throughout my life. Studying and documenting the behaviour of merlin and red-throated diver, long summer nights with seabirds on Hermaness, or cold winter days waiting for ravens to gather and feast on a carcass; time spent like this is hard to beat.

Good birding days are as much about the people I am with and the location we are in, as the birds we actually find. True for most birders, nostalgia plays a huge part in my time in the field. A North Isles man through and through, nowhere do I feel a greater connection than in Unst, Fetlar and Yell. So many things connect me to these islands but it is what separates them that tantalises me the most: Bluemull Sound. Often referred to by Shetland Bird Club as the 'Bluemull Triangle', this remarkable body of water fringes the shores of these and the many small islands in between, where the daily rhythm of the tides rip and roar through, supporting as rich a diversity beneath the surface as it does above.

It would be impossible to even guess at how many thousands of hours I have spent on Bluemull. The ferry service that underpins island living, and my time as a crew member on board, would alone amount to a significant percentage of my life. Over the years I've spent a great deal of time on various different boats here too. I have few more precious memories than the times I was lucky to tag along with the late Bobby Tulloch. His own love and knowledge of these waters definitely fuelled my own. It is a rare day when, out now on my own boat, I don't pass a place or species which makes me think of him.

Long-tailed ducks *(Clangula hyemalis)*, Bluemull, © Brydon Thomason.

My time working on otters sees me following the rhythm of the tides here too, with many of my favourite ranges spanning the perimeter of these Sounds. All my most epic cetacean encounters have also been here, from breaching humpback whales to seal-hunting orca; but the bird life, no matter the season, is even more special.

A 'seabird highway' throughout the summer months, small feeding parties of auks and gannets commute through the Sound around the clock. Used similarly as a flyway during migration, I've picked up various species from the ferry, sometimes battling into a gale force wind; both sooty and Manx shearwaters, European and Leach's storm petrel, pomarine and long-tailed skua, grey phalarope, surf scoter and even black tern and Franklin's gull. The latter though, however exciting it sounds, is one of many identification mistakes made and learned from over the years. First put out as a laughing gull, I soon saw the irony involved ...

But winter is the season when Bluemull comes even further into its own. The congregations of wintering eider and long-tailed duck are a spectacle in themselves. Over 1,000 of the charismatic and onomatopoeically named 'calloo' spend the winter here. This count is even more impressive through late winter onwards as birds that have wintered elsewhere arrive to use the area as a pre-breeding staging post, when up to 1,200 (the largest in the UK) can be seen in a single flock, soon to be northward bound for the Arctic summer.

King eider *(Somateria spectabilis)* with eiders, Bluemull, © Brydon Thomason.

'Dunter' numbers are usually at their highest during mid to late winter, numbering well over 1,000, often broken into multiple flocks but sometimes in one great, gregarious feeding frenzy. This melee of black, white and brown over the winter water is easily one of the most captivating spectacles of the year for me.

Within these flocks there is even greater excitement. A flash of baby blue from out amongst the black capped commoners or a blaze of orange, glimpsed through the clustered olive-toned 'nebs', is what inspires systematic scanning of these flocks. More king eiders have been recorded here than at any other site in Shetland, possibly even Britain. Whether it's the dazzling splendour of a drake, the subtle detail of a prince or the more refined and modest beauty of a queen, there are few more exhilarating discoveries – until I pick out that Dresser's or Pacific, that is …

Perhaps, however, even more so than this track record, the Bluemull Triangle has form for another high Arctic seabird – white-billed diver. Although there has been a considerable increase in records over recent years, there are still few finer winter sites than focusing your optics onto that pale open face, holding aloft an ivory-toned bill. Each and every one I see stirs nostalgia, taking my thoughts right back to finding my first nearly 30 years ago: gazing in awe through my trusty Bushnell Spacemaster from Odsta, Fetlar, on one of those beautifully crisp and calm mid-winter days in January 1993, noting its bulk on the water, thick-set neck and neon-like glow of its characteristic bill in my description for BBRC, I could never have imagined just how much their status would change in the years ahead.

Continuing the winter Arctic vagrant theme that it is so renowned for, it was here at

Ivory gull *(Pagophila eburnea)*, Fetlar, December 2008, © Brydon Thomason, "Over the waves, through the winds and along the shores, Bluemull funnelled in this holy grail of winter birding."

this very same site, in December 2008, that the shores of Bluemull featured as the location for one of my most rewarding and, surely, once in a lifetime discoveries – the enigmatic ivory gull. Over the waves, through the winds and along the shores, Bluemull funnelled in this holy grail of winter birding. I wonder and, must admit, hope that eventually one day it will do the same for me with a Ross's, but even without one, it will always be Bluemull for my best day's birding.

Tengtastic: Tengmalm's owls

2019/20

Phil Harris

On 19th February 2019 we were sitting in the kitchen at Rebecca's parents' home in Suffolk, on a winter break from Shetland, when the rare bird WhatsApp alert went off on both our phones. I was first to read: "Tengmalm's owl at Tumblin!" We both just sat in silence and disbelief; one of the birds we had dreamed of seeing when we moved to Shetland was now just a 20-minute drive from our home and we were not there.

One hundred years since the last Shetland record we had to take action, but with the family break set to continue for another two weeks, and a three-year-old daughter, it was not going to be easy. That night I was on the road to Aberdeen, booked on a mid-morning flight back to Shetland but hoping I might get on the first flight; Becca was going to wait for me to return and then travel up.

No space on the early flight meant I arrived in Shetland just before lunch. Little did I know that Roger Riddington was in the same predicament, having left Shetland for a winter break in Italy. We both arrived at Tumblin to hear the news that there was no sign so far, however the plan after we arrived was that myself and Roger would be allowed to crawl under the pine plantation to see if we could relocate it.

To cut a long story short there was no sign of it. I had planned to stay the night in Shetland so I had the next day, but Roger was due to fly out again that afternoon. Our next chance would be dusk so Roger hatched a new plan to get the last flight from Shetland, then take my car from Aberdeen back to Edinburgh for his flight from Edinburgh. There was no sign at dusk – damn!

The following morning I arrived at Tumblin with little hope, and was met by approximately 100 birders! The owner only wanted one person (me) to enter the garden to search for the bird. So with all eyes on me I began crawling on my back under the pines. After about three metres I looked up and was looking at the backside of a Tengmalm's owl; I will never forget the moment when it looked down at me with those incredible eyes. I exited the plantation like a ferret only to realise I had no idea which tree it was in! I just started blurting out, "It is in there."

Of course birders wanted to get in but I was under strict instructions from the owner, so after a bit of negotiation we managed to set up a viewpoint and get views of the bird. Phew!

Rebecca flew up the following day and got the job of searching under the pines but there was no sign. Fortunately, later that day the bird was relocated 2.5km away at Lea Gardens where she watched it consuming a ringed plover. The bird was last reported at Lea Gardens on 2nd March.

Little did I know that this would not be my last Tengmalm's encounter: it got better and better.

We returned to Shetland in late March and on 3rd April I had a spare hour so decided to visit Lea Gardens to look for long-eared owls. I stepped out of the car and was immediately aware of ravens and hooded crows dive-bombing something on a hill in the distance. I looked through my bins and saw an adult white-tailed eagle! I ran to inform Rosa and James, the owners of Lea Gardens, and we quickly drove up the peat track and got amazing views of the eagle.

On returning I only had 20 minutes so had a quick walk around. Just as I was coming to the end I walked under a sparse pine tree; I don't know why but I looked directly up and 'boom', there were those incredible eyes staring back at me, giving far better views than I had previously. After some negotiation the gardens were opened up for visiting birders to enjoy the owl. The bird showed well on the Friday/Saturday but I couldn't find it on the Sunday morning: unbelievably it had relocated to Unst!

I spent many great days observing the bird and studying its behaviour: prey included redshank, ringed plover, blackbird and chaffinch, which after dashing out of its roost it caught on the ground in front of visiting birders.

We assumed that was the end of the Tengmalm's story, but fast forward to February 2020. Brydon Thomason was alerted by a friend about a Tengmalm's owl he had photographed in December in the Lyndsey Lea plantation at Kergord whilst on a training exercise with the coastguard.

Two months had passed but I decided the next day to carry out a search of the Kergord valley. I spent the best part of the day searching all the plantations and Lea Gardens but there was no sign. My last resort was to go back to Lyndsey Lea at dusk in the hope of locating it hunting. I arrived about 40 minutes before last light, just as a heavy hail shower came in, and asked myself whether this was a good idea. Just then a wren began to alarm from some dense larch trees; I went in to investigate and there were those incredible yellow eyes staring at me once again.

The bird was back in the same roost the following day, giving views down to a few feet. Obviously, birders started to speculate about it being the 2019 Tumblin bird. Given that there had not been any records for 100 years this seemed plausible, however the bird was caught and ringed and was found to be a first-winter due to the single generation of flight feathers. So two birds in Shetland had been located just a few kilometres apart!

I again followed this bird every day, and observed it with prey including blackbird, robin and goldcrest plus field mice. It would cache prey during the day low down in forks of trees, then return for them at dusk when I could approach to just a few feet whilst it consumed its prey. This bird was confirmed as a male by its DNA, and although there is no proof it is thought that the first bird was a female based on the larger prey items and a Finnish expert believing it to be female on the colouring of the face.

Incredibly this bird also relocated to Lea Gardens and was observed in the same trees as the first bird. Even more incredibly both birds left, presumably for Norway, on 14th April.

My mission now is to find my own.

Editorial comment: *More detailed information about these remarkable occurrences can be found in:*

Harris, P.A. 2020. Roosting and feeding behaviour of Shetland Tengmalm's Owls in 2019 and 2020. Scot. Birds 40: 278-281

Harris, P.A. 2021. Two Tengmalm's Owls in Shetland. Shetland Bird Report 2019: 147-152

Tengmalm's owl *(Aegolius funereus)*, Tresta, March 2020, © Rebecca Nason.

References and further reading

Bedford, Mary, Duchess of. 1937. *A Bird-watcher's Diary*. Privately published.

Brown, J. Manx Shearwater: extinct in Shetland? *Shetland Bird Report* 2018: 131-133

Clarke, W.E. 1912. *Studies in Bird Migration*. Volume 2. Gurney & Jackson, Edinburgh.

Conlin, A. 2019. Great Knot, Unst, 30 May-4 June 2019 – the second record for Shetland. *Scot. Birds* 39: 368-371

Cooper, D. & Kay, B. 2018. Marmora's Warbler, Baliasta, Unst, 14 May 2018 – the first record for Shetland. *Scot. Birds* 38: 360-363

Coutts, D. 2019. Seven owls in Shetland. *Scot. Birds* 39: 252-258

Del Hoyo, J. *et al.* 1996. *Handbook of the Birds of the World*. Vol. 3. Hoatzin to Auks. Lynx Editions, Barcelona.

Dierschke, J. *et al.* 2011. *Die Vogelwelt der Insel Helgoland*. OAG Helgoland, Helgoland.

Ellis, P.M. 1992. Great Knot: new to Britain and Ireland. *Brit. Birds* 85: 426-428

Forrester, R.W. *et al.* 2007. *The Birds of Scotland*. SOC, Aberlady.

Gear, S. 1983. *Foula: Island West of the Sun*. Robert Hale, London.

Harris, P.A. 2020. Roosting and feeding behaviour of Shetland Tengmalm's Owls in 2019 and 2020. *Scot. Birds* 40: 278-281

Harris, P.A. 2021. Two Tengmalm's Owls in Shetland. *Shetland Bird Report* 2019: 147-152

Harrop, A.H.J. 2010. Records of Hawk Owls in Britain. *Brit. Birds* 103: 276-283

Jamieson, R.A. 1986. *Thin Wealth*. Polygon, Edinburgh.

Martin, J.R & Mikkola, H. 2019. Distribution trends of the Scops Owl in Britain and northern Europe. *Scot. Birds* 39: 168-172

Miles, W. 2014. Swinhoe's Petrels in summer 2013; the first and second for Fair Isle. *Fair Isle Bird Observatory Report for 2013*: 112-117

Miles, W. *et al.* 2014. Results of biometric, sound and DNA analyses of two Swinhoe's Petrels on Fair Isle in 2013 and diagnosis of breeding status. *Fair Isle Bird Observatory Report for 2013*: 117-120

Mitchell *et al.* 2004. *Seabird Populations of Britain and Ireland*. T & AD Poyser, London.

Pennington, M. *et al.* 2004. *The Birds of Shetland*. Christopher Helm, London.

Preston, D. 2018. White-winged Scoter, Yell & Unst, 16-22 October 2017 – third Scottish record and first for Shetland. *Scot. Birds* 38: 82-83

Robertson, I.S. 1975. Ovenbird in Shetland. *Brit. Birds* 68: 453-455

Robinson, M. & Becker, C.D. 1986. Snowy Owls on Fetlar. *Brit. Birds* 79: 228-242

Saxby, H.L. 1874. *The Birds of Shetland*. Maclachlan & Stewart, Edinburgh.

Slack, R. 2009. *Rare Birds: Where and When*. Rare Birds Books, York.

Smith, M. *et al.* 2014. Geolocator tagging reveals Pacific migration of Red-necked Phalarope Phalaropus lobatus breeding in Scotland. *Ibis* 156: 870-873

Smith, M. *et al.* 2018. Further evidence of transatlantic migration routes and Pacific wintering grounds of Red-necked Phalaropes breeding in Shetland. *Brit. Birds* 111: 428-437

Svanbarg, S. & Waldenstrom, J. 2011. Population fluctuations and timing of spring migration of the Scandinavian Bluethroat at Ottenby Bird Observatory, Sweden, 1955-2008. *Ornis Svecica* 21: 92-100

Tulloch, R.J. 1968. Snowy Owls breeding in Shetland in 1967. *Brit. Birds* 61: 119-132

Williamson, K. 1965. *Fair Isle and its Birds*. Oliver & Boyd, Edinburgh.

Wynn, R.B. *et al.* 2014. Spring migration routes of Long-tailed Skuas around and across the UK – results of observational and tracking data. *Brit. Birds* 107: 220-228

Editors' Biographies

Andrew Harrop has been an active birder for more than 50 years, during which time he has served on both local and national records committees, including a term as chair of BOURC (the body which maintains the British List of birds). He is co-author of *The Birds of Leicestershire and Rutland* and author of *Rutland Butterfly Atlas*. Since retiring to Shetland he has devoted much of his spare time to sound recording birds. He has also discovered both White's thrush and bluetail, and is looking forward to discovering a rubythroat.

Rebecca Nason is an award-winning wildlife photographer, naturalist, author and birder originally from Cambridge but now living the dream in Lerwick with her young family, having been hooked on the Shetland Islands since being assistant warden in Fair Isle in 2003 and 2004. She owns Shetland Seabird Tours – The Noss Boat – with Phil Harris, runs a small B&B, carries out bird surveys, bird ringing and is currently enjoying being a judge for WildArt Photographer of the Year and Scottish Nature Photography Awards. She is fiercely competitive and always after that special "one shot" to quench the frustratingly unquenchable photographic and artistic thirst!

BV - #0068 - 210323 - C134 - 240/165/8 - PB - 9781910997451 - Matt Lamination

Monster Sitter

'Monster Sitter'

An original concept by Jenny Jinks

Illustrated by Ardhi Al Hafiz

Published by MAVERICK ARTS PUBLISHING LTD

Suite 1, Hillreed House, 54 Queen Street,

Horsham, West Sussex, RH13 5AD

+44 (0)1403 256941

A CIP catalogue record for this book is available at the British Library.

ISBN 978-1-83511-075-1

Printed in India

Maverick publishing

www.maverickbooks.co.uk

Purple

This book is rated as: Purple Band (Guided Reading)

Monster Sitter

By Jenny Jinks

Illustrated by
Ardhi Al Hafiz

Samiar stared through the shop window at the Rocket Board—the best skateboard in the world. 'If only I could afford one,' Samiar thought, looking at his tatty old board.

But it was no use. He had been saving his pocket money for weeks, but he still had nowhere near enough. At this rate he would be 100 before he could afford a Rocket Board.

On his way home, Samiar spotted a poster on the noticeboard outside the supermarket.

It said:

SITTER WANTED FOR

OUR TWO LOVELY

LITTLE MONSTERS.

Please call if interested.

Samiar couldn't believe his luck. This was just what he needed! He had looked after his baby cousin before. All she did was sleep. This would be easy!

Samiar phoned the number on the poster and explained that he was interested in the job. "Great!" said a woman on the other end. "Can you come this evening?"

Later that day, Samiar skated up to a big, old house on the outskirts of town. He knocked on the door. CREEEAK! The door swung open, but nobody was there. Samiar had a bad feeling about this.

"Welcome!" A tall man with shaggy hair hurried down the stairs. "I'm Mr Howler. Luna and Wilf are tucked up in bed."

"Help yourself to anything you need. Hopefully they won't be any trouble," Mrs Howler said, giving a nervous glance up the stairs. "Just... try not to disturb them."

"Gosh, it's late, the moon is already up. We really must go," said Mr Howler as they ran out of the front door. "Good luck!"

Samiar nervously stepped inside.

The house looked perfectly normal on the inside.

Maybe everything would be alright after all.

All was quiet, so he settled himself on the sofa, ready to watch some TV. This was going to be the easiest job ever!

THUD!

Samiar heard a noise coming from upstairs.

THUD! THUD! THUD!

He ran up the stairs and opened the bedroom door. Luna and Wilf were wide awake, bouncing on their beds.

"You should be asleep!" Samiar told them.

"Not tired," said Luna.

"Big moon!" said Wilf.

Samiar pulled the curtains to block the light from the full moon. Then he tucked them both back into bed.

Samiar was just settling back down on the sofa when he heard giggling behind him.

He spun around just in time to see Luna creeping downstairs.

"What are you doing?" Samiar asked.

"You're supposed to be asleep!"

He picked Luna up and carried her back up the stairs.

Was it his imagination or was she hairier than she had been before?

Samiar was tucking Luna into bed when he noticed Wilf wasn't there.

Where had he gone?!

He heard rustling from downstairs.

Samiar raced down to the kitchen.

"Stop!" Samiar cried.

Wilf was chewing on a cardboard box.

"Hungry!" cried Wilf.

"No snacks," said Samiar. "It's bedtime."

He picked Wilf up and carried him back upstairs.

Was it his imagination or were Wilf's teeth pointier than before?

Finally, both Wilf and Luna were settled back into bed.

Samiar sat back down with a sigh. But then...

"HOOOOOOWL!"

Was that Luna and Wilf?

Were they... howling?!

Samiar crept up the stairs.

Quietly, he pushed open the bedroom door...

and gasped.

Luna and Wilf were sitting on the windowsill

howling at the moon.

And they were both covered in hair!

Samiar quickly pulled the door shut again.

They were WEREWOLVES!

The door handle began to rattle.

Samiar held it shut. He couldn't let them out.

They might be dangerous.

The door kept rattling.

He didn't know what to do. He was stuck in a house with two werewolves!

Soon, the rattling stopped, and the howls stopped too.

Samiar listened at the door. Now all he could hear was quiet sobs.

They were crying.

Samiar started to feel bad. They were only little.

How much harm could they do?

Carefully, slowly, he opened the door.

Wilf and Luna were sitting sadly on the rug.

They didn't look dangerous at all.

"Do you want to come downstairs for a bit?"

Samiar asked.

Both their little faces brightened.

Downstairs, Samiar decided to make them a snack. He didn't really know what werewolves liked to eat. He found a box of biscuits.

They gobbled the lot, and the box too!

“Bedtime,” Samiar said when they had finished.

“HOOOOOWWWWWLLLLL!”

“Alright, alright, you can stay up a bit longer. Just stop howling!” Samiar said.

But what was he supposed to do with two werewolf kids?

“Do you want to have a ride on my skateboard?” Samiar asked.

Luna and Wilf nodded excitedly.

“Weeeee!” they cried as they whizzed back and forth down the hall.

Finally, Luna and Wilf started to look tired.

Luna let out a big yawn.

"Time for bed," said Samiar. He led Luna and Wilf back up the stairs, tucked them into bed and read them a story. Before he was finished, they were already snoring gently.

A while later, Mr and Mrs Howler came home.

"Glad to see you're still in one piece!" Mr Howler joked. "I hope they weren't any trouble."

Samiar smiled. "Not at all," he said. "Actually, they were a lot of fun."

Mr Howler handed Samiar his money.

"Our friends are looking for a sitter too," he said. "If you can handle our little monsters then they should be no trouble."

Samiar couldn't wait. If he kept this up, he would be able to buy the Rocket Board in no time.

Samiar babysat for all of the Howlers' friends. Samiar never knew what weird and wonderful family he was going to walk into next, but every evening was a new adventure.

Samiar had soon earned enough money to buy his Rocket Board. But he kept doing his job. His new board made zooming around town from one job to the next even more fun.

Samiar loved his new job, and he became the number one monster sitter in town.

Quiz

1. How did Samiar find out about the babysitting job?

a) His mum told him about it

b) A poster

c) The newspaper

2. What were the names of the werewolf children?

a) Wilf and Luna

b) Wolf and Lily

c) Will and Lola

3. How did Samiar tire the children out?

a) He had them tidy the house

b) He had them run a race

c) He let them ride on his skateboard

4. What did Samiar do when tucking the children into bed?

a) He sang to them

b) He danced for them

c) He read them a story

5. Who did Samiar babysit for next?

a) His family

b) Mr and Mrs Howler's friends

c) His neighbours

Turn over for answers

Book Bands for Guided Reading

The Institute of Education book banding system is a scale of colours that reflects the various levels of reading difficulty. The bands are assigned by taking into account the content, the language style, the layout and phonics. Word, phrase and sentence level work is also taken into consideration.

Maverick Early Readers are a bright, attractive range of books covering the pink to white bands. All of these books have been book banded for guided reading to the industry standard and edited by a leading educational consultant.

To view the whole Maverick Readers scheme, visit our website at www.maverickearlyreaders.com

Or scan the QR code above to view our scheme instantly!

Quiz Answers: 1b, 2a, 3c, 4c, 5b